Addiction-Proof
PARENTING

*Biblical
Prevention
Strategies*

MARK E. SHAW

Addiction-Proof Parenting
Biblical Prevention Strategies

by Mark Shaw

Scripture quotations are from The Holy Bible, English Standard
Version®, copyright ©2001 by Crossway Bibles, a publishing
ministry of Good News Publishers. Used by permission and where
noted, The King James Version and The New King James Version.

Cover design by Melanie Schmidt

ISBN 13: 978-1-885904-88-1
ISBN 10: 1-885904-88-6

PRINTED IN THE UNITED STATES OF AMERICA
BY
FOCUS PUBLISHING
Bemidji, Minnesota

In biblical Christianity it is not enough that we stop doing what is wrong; we must also start doing what is right, and for the right reasons. The "put-off, put-on by changing the way you think" principle is taught clearly in Ephesians 4:22-24. Here is a book that masterfully helps parents do that personally and with their children. The practical suggestions reveal the author's experience as a parent, pastor and counselor. This book will be helpful both with parents-to-be and those with children enslaved to life-dominating sins. Thanks, Mark!

Randy Patten, Executive Director
National Association of Nouthetic Counselors (NANC)

As a pastor and counselor I encounter parents almost weekly who are baffled by their child's excursion into the wilderness of addiction. Mark Shaw provides a biblically-based parenting handbook of preventative measures. I refer to this as *engagement parenting*. This is not a "Just Say No" campaign. Shaw teaches parents how to say yes to engaged parenting that will produce kids who *want* to say no to addictive substances.

Dr. Howard Eyrich, Briarwood Counseling Ministries
President Emeritus, Birmingham Theological Seminary

As a parent who made all the mistakes listed in this book, I wish it had been presented to me decades ago. It is painful to see it carried on into the next generation. I would implore young parents to read and heed this valuable resource in the light of our culture today, and call upon the strength of God's Holy Spirit to guide them in their parenting skills. The final Appendix D (God's Grace for Parents who think they have failed) offers hope for my generation.

Name Withheld

Dedication

To some of the best parents I've ever known:

Michael and Paula Fargarson

Mark and Darby Travers

Charlie and Martha Willcox

and

Ronny and Sandra Shaw

Addiction-Proof Parenting
Prevention Strategies for Parents
Table of Contents

Page

Introduction
Why I Wrote *Addiction-Proof Parenting*

Section 1: General Biblical Parenting Principles
1. The Problem   3
2. The Good News   9
3. Who is Responsible?   17
4. Discipline in Love   25
5. The Rod and Reproof   33
6. Physical Touch and Praise   45
7. A Balanced Approach   49

Section 2: The Biblical Approach to "Addiction"
8. Understanding "Addiction"   61
9. What a Transformation Looks Like   71
10. Understanding Addictive Thinking   75
11. How to Raise an "Addict"   83

Section 3: Specific Addiction-Proof Parenting Principles
12. The Entitlement Mentality   93
13. Be Humble   99
14. The Consumer Mentality   105
15. Be Giving   113
16. The Victim Mentality   117
17. Too Much Responsibility   127
18. Too Little Responsibility   133
19. Be Responsible (Obedient)   149
20. The Perishing Mentality   157
21. Be Grateful (Joy)   163
22. The Rebellious Mentality   169
23. Be Submissive   177
24. Conclusion   185

Appendices

		Page
Appendix A:	The Whole Story	191
Appendix B:	Knowledge, Understanding and Wisdom	199
Appendix C:	Mark and Mary's Tips for Parents	201
Appendix D:	God's Grace for Parents Who Think They Have Failed	205

Introduction

Ask yourself this question: "Am I raising an 'addict' of some type right now?"

You reaction might be, "What an awful question! Of course not! I am an excellent parent." But think about this: what if God allowed you to look into the future to see how your child would turn out as an adult?

If God did allow you to look into the future and you saw that your child or grandchild would actually be an "addict" of some type (i.e. gambling, drunkenness, pornography, idolatry, and the like), what would you change now? Do you have any idea?

I've got great news. This book will answer that question for you and enable you to implement some practical strategies to foster your child's thinking to prevent "addiction." The best part of it will be that these strategies will come directly and indirectly from the Word of God, which is not silent on this subject! God speaks loudly and clearly on this topic and wants you to trust Him.

Now, let me ask the question of you: "Are you raising an 'addict'?" You might respond in the following ways:

"It is impossible to know the future. I certainly *hope* I am not raising an 'addict'?"

Or sadly, would you say, "Yes, it seems that I am" or "It seems that I have"?

No one can predict if a child will grow up to be an "addict" of some kind. I'm not talking about genetics or physiological reasons for addiction. As of this writing, no one has discovered an "addiction gene" and there is no compelling evidence linking addiction to a brain disease or disorder (though secularists are calling it a brain disease now). I am not suggesting that upbringing and childhood environment are entirely responsible for becoming an addict. A child becomes addicted by personal choice and is one hundred percent responsible for the first choice to abuse an addictive substance (even if prescribed by a physician for legitimate physical reasons such as pain).

What I am suggesting is that your parenting skills (or lack thereof) have a direct impact upon your children. There is no question about the powerful influence that parents have upon the thinking of their

God-given children. A child's thinking and interpretations of life's events impact the decisions they make as adults. The Lord wants you to teach your child His Word and He promises blessing in this life and in the life to come when you do. Children learn spiritual truths by watching and listening to how their parents apply them to their lives.

In the movie, *Fireproof*, one of the actors is disillusioned and struggling in his marriage when he says to his friend, "Marriages are not fireproof. Sometimes you get burned." To which the other actor responded encouragingly, "Fireproof doesn't mean that fire will never come. But that when it comes, you will be able to withstand it."[1]

Likewise, addiction-proof parenting does not mean that temptations to use drugs will not occur in your child's lifetime. We are to be *in* the world but not *of* the world (John 17:16-21). *Addiction-Proof Parenting* means that when temptations come, your child will be ready for those challenges because of God's grace through your parenting investment. Your children can be addiction-proof by God's grace through your faithfulness to teach them to be obedient to His Word.

Whether your child is two years old, twelve years old, thirty-two years old, or even sixty-two years of age, it is not too late to begin gaining insights into how parenting impacts a young person's thinking, speaking, and doing. I will draw on the Word of God and my nearly twenty years of experience with addicts to provide clarity and wisdom to help you identify problematic patterns of parenting and replace them with good, biblical parenting techniques. My prayer is that this book will surprise you and be a tremendous resource to you by providing practical wisdom from God's Word to improve your parenting skills for the glory of God and the benefit of your child.

This book is not designed to be a list of do's and don'ts. While there are do's and don'ts in this book, my desire is for you to learn how to love your child by teaching your child to think, speak, and act according to God's Word of truth. This book is a call for you to present the grace and truth of God's Word to your children relationally so they will ultimately come to know the Lord Jesus Christ intimately and personally.

---

[1] "Fireproof", Provident Films, Sherwood Baptist Church, 2009.

Book Structure and Overview

The first section of this book contains general, basic biblical wisdom for all parents. This portion of the book will be especially helpful for new parents with very young children. Each chapter will end with key ideas and practical "To Do" suggestions so you can begin working with your child immediately.

The next section presents basic concepts in the biblical approach to addiction. For example, did you know that the word "addiction" is the world's term for the problem? Biblically, the problem is idolatry, which encompasses every type of "addiction." Nonetheless, when the word "addiction" is used in this book, its definition will always be slightly modified to mean the following definition in my book *The Heart of Addiction*: "addiction is defined as the 'persistent *habitual* use of a substance known by the user to be harmful.'"[2] Think of the problem of addiction (idolatry) as habitual rather than compulsive and you will better capture its biblical meaning.

The second section will also present a brief overview of the biblical approach to addiction, a satirical look at how to raise an addict to illustrate what NOT to do as a parent, and introduce you to five basic *mentalities* of an addict. These mentalities are based upon two passages of Scripture: Matthew 22:27-40 and Ephesians 5:18-21.

In the third and final section, you will learn how addicts develop selfish thinking patterns and the five mentalities which must replace them. *Addiction-Proof Parenting* hinges upon changing your child's thinking to be more Christ-centered rather than self-centered, which will produce godly responses in how your child emotes and acts. As a parent, think how pleased you will be when you hear and see godliness, righteousness, love, respect, and tender-heartedness in your child's words and actions!

Mark Shaw

---

[2] Shaw, Mark, *The Heart of Addiction*, Focus Publishing, Bemidji, MN, p. 28. In all honesty, I do not prefer the word "addiction" because it is a worldly term that can be misleading; however, that is the word that most people are familiar with. The biblical word for "addiction" is "idolatry", but that word is unfortunately confusing to many. My hope is that you will embrace those biblical words by the end of this book as you gain more understanding. In the meantime, please understand that "addiction" will be defined as "habitual" any time it is used in this book so that it is more in line with biblical concepts.

Why I Wrote *Addiction-Proof Parenting*

There are several programs that exist today intended to combat the increasingly dangerous and devastating problem of teenage substance abuse, illicit sexual activities, and addictions in general. While some of these programs offer helpful suggestions, I believe they are missing the heart of the problem. These programs address externals by focusing almost exclusively upon the environment, outside pressures, stressors, biological predispositions, and poor parenting while omitting the internal heart attitudes of these addicted young people who are ultimately responsible for their poor decisions and choices. My friends, God is not silent on this issue, yet He seems to be ignored by even so-called Christian approaches. God is speaking to us by His Spirit through His Word of truth, but are we listening?

Although not dealing with addiction directly, one example of a program that did not "work" (because they not only had the wrong goal but also the wrong means to achieve it) was developed by the governing leaders in one U.S. city who wanted to improve low test scores of their students. They poured billions of dollars into the school system according to this article by the CATO Institute:

> Kansas City spent as much as $11,700 per pupil – more money per pupil, on a cost of living adjusted basis, than any other of the 280 largest districts in the country. The money bought higher teachers' salaries, 15 new schools, and such amenities as an Olympic-sized swimming pool with an underwater viewing room, television and animation studios, a robotics lab, a 25-acre wildlife sanctuary, a zoo, a model United Nations with simultaneous translation capability, and field trips to Mexico and Senegal. The student-teacher ratio was 12 or 13 to 1, the lowest of any major school district in the country.
>
> The results were dismal. Test scores did not rise ... The Kansas City experiment suggests that, indeed, educational problems can't be solved by throwing

money at them, that the structural problems of our current educational system are far more important than a lack of material resources, and that the focus on desegregation diverted attention from the real problem, low achievement.[1]

Like this program in Kansas City, most addiction prevention programs focus upon external changes rather than addressing the real issues of the heart. Do you know why? One reason is that they do not know what the heart of the problem is. I want to let you in on a little secret: the heart of addiction is sin. "Addiction" is actually a worldly term and a misnomer because the biblical names are idolatry, sin, sorcery, drunkenness, and rebellion, but those are strong terms for an American culture that chooses to ignore the problem rather than face the reality of sin and its consequences.

You can choose to stop reading this book and stick your head in the sand, but the problem will not magically go away because you ignore it. Satan wants your child to die and go to hell. On the path to hell, Satan's desire is for your child to experience misery disguised as escape and stress relief. A stress-free life is not the goal. Hell is a real place (Matthew 8:12; Matthew 24:51; Revelation 20:15) and the consequences from poor choices to use drugs or take part in other addictive pleasures often end in death. Likewise, the consequence of a lack of parenting is death, too, since a child left alone will choose to walk a path of trusting in himself leading to a myriad of problems like addiction, divorce, disease, pain, suffering, and ultimately death (Proverbs 13:15).

Focusing on these severe consequences and the reality of hell are not enough to fix the problem. They get your attention, but are based in fear. God wants you to be aware of these realities but He greatly desires for you to have faith in Him to work in your situation as a parent. The good news is that your faith to trust Him will empower you to do something about the problem. By trusting God, I mean that you can pray, read His Word, change your thinking, and do what He requires of parents in accordance with His Word under the power of

---

[1] Article by the CATO Institute at http://www.cato.org/pubs/pas/pa-298.html. Note: This article mentions a similar initiative in Sausalito, CA, that failed, too.

the Holy Spirit. God has given you the responsibility of pointing your child to back to Him—your child's Perfect Father.

Those who claim to have answers outside of these spiritual realities do not have any real answers because their hope is in money and external changes rather than in Christ. Furthermore, with worldly thinking, people blame everyone and everything but themselves. Some in the world even blame God! The world looks for power in itself but not in God. Yet the Bible is different. The Word of God has answers because it is the spoken words of truth applied to our lives. The hope of the world is the Lord Jesus Christ who works through His children (the church)[2] to bring hope and help to a dying world. Society's answer is to replace old school buildings with new ones and add all of the modern technological bells and whistles. But test scores of students do not improve and addictions do not disappear. Why? Because the answer is not found in externals but in real heart change that only Christ can produce by His grace.

When the heart is transformed, behaviors will change. This heart change must occur in both parents and in their children, all of whom are responsible for their own choices. This book will address the real heart of the issue from a biblical perspective with the hope that your thinking will be transformed. You and I are part of the problem if we refuse to listen to the Holy Spirit who speaks to us in accordance to His Word of truth. You and I are part of the problem if we hear the truth from the Holy Spirit but fail to act by putting changes into place. You and I are part of the problem if we fail to tell others about the real hope of the world for the problems of addictive thinking and behavior in young people.

Rather than microscope and analyze each type of addictive behavior and destructive activity Satan uses to tempt young people, I encourage you to learn the truth in God's Word. Billy Graham's wife once commented to a man who was in charge of identifying counterfeit money at Scotland Yard, "You must spend a lot of time handling counterfeit money to know what it looks like." "No," he replied. "We never touch the stuff. All day long, we just handle the

---

[2] Note: The church is not a building. It's the people of God who are "called out" of darkness and into His marvelous light.

real thing—genuine currency. And when a counterfeit bill comes our way—we can quickly detect it."[3] Rather than focus upon the externals, we need to focus on Christ and His Word of truth to learn how to effectively deal with the heart of the problem of addictions.

Counterfeits will come and go. Addictions will come and go. They will constantly change as Satan changes his temptation strategies. But one thing will never change: the Lord Jesus Christ and His eternal Word of truth found in the Bible. As you learn the truth, you will be able to recognize every counterfeit of Satan. The Bible is often a neglected resource for dealing with this problem yet when coupled with the Holy Spirit of God, it is an incredible weapon that transforms the rebellious heart of both parents and their children. Hebrews 4:12 summarizes the power of the Word of God: **"For the word of God is living and active, sharper than any two-edged sword, piercing to the division of soul and of spirit, of joints and of marrow, and discerning the thoughts and intentions of the heart."** God gets to the heart of the issue and we need Him to open our eyes and to provide us with His power to overcome this problem. Therefore, **"Let the word of Christ dwell in you richly in all wisdom, teaching and admonishing one another in psalms and hymns and spiritual songs, singing with grace in your hearts to the Lord."**[4]

Programs are not the answer. Even this book is not the answer. Going to church every Sunday is not the answer. New school buildings, new curriculums, and homeschooling are not the answer. While these are all good and helpful things, they alone are not sufficient in themselves. Only Christ is the answer. He alone is the only complete answer so you must depend upon Him to work through you to accomplish His Plans by His power. This book will simply point you to Him and His unchanging Word of truth.

Addiction-Proof Parenting is designed to teach you what God says about the nature of His character and the fallen nature of your character and that of your child for the purpose of glorifying God when He brings transforming heart change into your lives. When

---

[3] Excerpted from http://www.harvest.org/devotional/Index.php/2/2008/01/11.html Greg Laurie, Senior Pastor, Harvest Christian Fellowship in CA – daily devotions – from Jan. 11, 2008.
[4] Colossians 3:16.

the will is transformed by the power of Christ, then thoughts, words, and actions change, too. Parents who implement these strategies and address the heart of the problem in themselves and in their children will see God's glory magnified in front of their eyes. John 6:63-64 reminds us that human effort apart from the Holy Spirit is useless: **"It is the Spirit who gives life; the flesh is of no avail. The words that I have spoken to you are spirit and life. [64] But there are some of you who do not believe."** Do you believe God?

Believing is doing. Believing produces actions in accordance with His Word (James 1:22). The goal of parents must not be primarily to "fix" their children, but to glorify God by trusting in Him today. The goal is to trust that He will do what He says He will do in His Word through you by the power of His might—by the power of the Holy Spirit.

Section One

General Biblical Parenting Practices

Chapter 1
The Problem

Young Scott is being raised by his grandparents who love him very much. They feel sorry for "Scottie," as they call him, because his father died from an overdose of drugs and his mother is on crystal meth. Since they feel sorry for "Scottie," they tend to give him everything he wants. "Well, he doesn't see his parents so maybe we can give him the things he wants" is what his grandparents often think. (To be continued at the beginning of each chapter throughout this book…complete story can be read in Appendix A)

We are experiencing an epidemic in our country. While you may think I am writing about the drug and alcohol epidemic in our culture, there is actually a bigger problem than that: a lack of biblical parenting. Some of the symptoms of this malady are Christian teenagers leaving their faith in the college years, co-habitating with boyfriends or girlfriends, having babies outside of marriage, aborting unwanted pregnancies, living selfishly, and using or abusing drugs and alcohol at an alarming rate. Christian families are failing to do "addiction-proof parenting," as I call it, but in reality, it is simply a lack of *biblical* parenting.

Drugs and alcohol[3] are not the primary problem. The primary problem lies within the human hearts of parents and children who are unintentionally and unknowingly taught to live for self-centered pleasures and the avoidance of pain and suffering. We live in a culture where delayed gratification is a foreign concept to most children, *and even parents*. Drug users and abusers know very little about delayed gratification.

Couples who choose to have a family must realize the extent to which this will affect their lives. They must be committed to the long-term responsibilities involved in training children who truly belong to God who will hold them accountable for the way in which they parent. Following are some principles of parenting you must know as you embark on this journey.

<u>Parenting a child is not accomplished "in name only."</u> Many people today claim to be "parents" when they simply were involved

---

[3] Alcohol is a drug in liquid form but I separate it out simply because our culture views alcohol differently from drugs—though, again, alcohol is a drug.

in the reproductive process of the child but are no longer involved in the discipline and training process. Having a baby does not make anyone a productive, responsible parent. Changing diapers and feeding a baby are essential for the physical health of the child but there is much more to the calling of being a godly parent. Godly parents are concerned about the spiritual health of their children. As a child ages, there is more to being a responsible parent than physically paying for uniforms, books, sports activities, college, and a wedding. Most important, parenting a child involves spiritual responsibility.

Parenting a child must be sacrificial. It is costly in terms of time and money. Parents must purposefully invest their energies into their children's lives while they are young or they will pay for their children's poor choices as they grow older and more independent. Parents are going to pay a price either on the front end or the back end for the way they parent or fail to parent their children. The price tag is often more expensive later in life.

For example, a married couple may choose to sacrifice some material goods now to allow mom to stay home with their child for the purpose of instructing him for the first five crucial years of life. They may further choose to home school their child to allow more time in parenting, teaching, training, and disciplining them throughout the developmental years. Whether the choice is for the first five years of the child's life or for the first eighteen years, the sacrifice will mean that they must live on one income, which results in living in a smaller home, driving used cars, and dressing themselves and their child in less expensive or used clothing. Their pursuit of the so-called American dream of a big home, new cars, and new clothes must be set aside for the pursuit of God's plan and purpose for His glory. The sacrifices now to be home more by not working outside the home will pay long-term "dividends" spiritually, as their child has the opportunity to learn from the example of his parents that making godly choices will lead to blessings, and that making ungodly choices will lead to curses (Deuteronomy 28).

The choice is no guarantee of having godly children. For some families it is a definite financial necessity to have both parents work outside the home. "Quality time" was the buzz word in parenting in the 80's. "Just *be* around your children more and they will turn out better," has been the line of thinking. No. Parenting the way God intends is much more active than that. I would encourage an

4

intentional quality time. It is intentional training.

Be cautious about choosing to be sinfully busy with the cares of this world and failing to invest time and energy in the discipline and teaching process of your children. Parents who decide to neglect church attendance, church involvement, home worship times, family Bible studies, and the like will see long-term consequences. They may think their children will pick up spiritual principles from others outside the home, but they will be wrong the majority of the time. In fact, Dr. Voddie Baucum states:

> "According to researchers, between 70 and 88 percent of Christian teens are leaving the church by their second year in college. That's right, modern American Christianity has a failure rate somewhere around eight (almost nine) out of ten when it comes to raising children who continue in the faith. Imagine the alarm if nearly 90 percent of our children couldn't read when they left high school. There wouldn't be room enough at school board meetings to hold all of the irate parents."[4]

As an addictions counselor and biblical counselor to families, I counsel parents who are sacrificing their children on the idolatrous altar of greed and financial gain. They accrue huge amounts of money, houses, cars, and other material possessions; however, they are neglecting to teach their children about serving Christ. These parents eventually end up squandering their hard-earned cash on drug rehabs, medical bills stemming from sinful choices, and other selfish, poor choices that the "adult" child is making (like getting pregnant out of wedlock and bringing home a grandchild for them to raise). Years of hard work and financial savings are lost.

Parenting a child is active, not passive. It is a sacrificial investment of time and resources. A parent cannot take long periods of time "off" from this twenty-four-hour-per-day job. Parents must understand that God places the responsibility of raising their children in the areas of intellectual, physical, spiritual, and social development directly on them as parents, and in particular, the father. Ephesians 6:4 states:

---

[4] Baucham, Voddie Jr., *Family Driven Faith*, Crossway Books, Wheaton, IL, 2007, p. 10-11.

"Fathers, do not provoke your children to anger, but bring them up in the discipline and instruction of the Lord."[5] Children do not exist for parents but parents for the children, in order to develop them into their own personhood in relationship with the Lord.[6] The spiritual health of your child is just as important as his physical health.

Parenting a child is relational. Your child is looking to you to provide his spiritual, physical, social, and intellectual needs (Luke 2:52). Your job is to further point your child to God as the Provider of everything he needs and teach him that you as a parent are simply the conduit through which God provides for His children. Your child's understanding of God will be impacted by the way you treat him. We all get a proper understanding of God as our Heavenly Parent from His Word of truth, but in the beginning of life parents reflect the love of God as they live out the command to love their children sacrificially, in the same way that God loves us through the sacrifice of His Son.

Parenting has a price tag, one that you must pay now or later. This bears repeating: Biblical parenting now is less costly than the price you may pay financially and emotionally with your child later in life. You determine the price you will pay. Will you invest in your child's upbringing and live sacrificially now as the Lord Jesus Christ did for His children? Will you sacrifice your time and energies to invest in the discipleship of your child now? Jesus did. He poured His life into twelve men. He lived with them. He ate with them. He walked with them. He challenged them intellectually as their "rabbi" or teacher. He provided for their physical needs. He cultivated His relationship with them. He instructed them about social relationships and the culture around them. He discipled them so that they would spiritually grow to become the great men of God they became after He ascended to heaven. Is your call to parenting any different than His call to disciple twelve men?

---

[5] Unless otherwise noted, all Scripture references are taken from *The Holy Bible: English Standard Version*. 2001 (electronic edition). Good News Publishers: Wheaton.

[6] The Reformation Study Bible, NKJV, R.C. Sproul, General Editor, Thomas Nelson Publishers, Nashville, TN, 1995, p. 1870.

KEY IDEAS AND PRACTICAL THINGS TO DO

1. Slow down your life by giving up an expendable hobby, project, or extraneous activity in order to carve out at least thirty minutes each day to spend teaching and talking with your child about the things of God in a natural way.

2. Send your child the message "I love you" and "I value you" by spending time with them rather than spending that time on a computer or in isolation from your child in some activity. Your influence upon the child is for a limited time.

3. Have a weekly (or daily) family worship and devotion time in your home where you pray, read God's Word, and sing a few praise songs.

Chapter 2
The Good News

At school, young "Scottie" is known simply as "Scott." This day Scott quickly darts out of his last class and heads toward the school gymnasium. A circle of his best friends are standing there and they welcome him to the group. He talks to them for just a little while before heading behind the gym. Scott knows he doesn't have much time to meet Derrick before catching his school bus home to his grandparents' house. Behind their school gym, Scott sells a bag of marijuana to Derrick who quickly hides it in his backpack...

Whether you realize it or not, there is a definite connection between the Gospel message and parenting. In fact, the Gospel must be woven into the very fabric of your parenting beginning at age 0. Yes, age 0.[7] One of your primary goals as a parent should be to point your child to the example set by the Lord Jesus Christ, who lived His life for the glory of God, the only perfect Parent. These lessons must begin very early in your child's life.

One day, one of my children whacked a younger sibling in the head with a toy when the younger one attempted to grab it without permission. The older child yelled "No!" and then—whack! The toy went right across the younger one's head. I was shocked and angry as I ran across the room to address the conflict. How could two people I love so much be so terribly mean and selfish to each other?

Why was I surprised? The Bible clearly teaches that we are all born with a sinful nature, meaning that without instruction a child will choose to please self rather than to please God. All children desire to be kings of their own little kingdoms and when someone fails to conform to their little kingdom rules, the child will punish the offender as he sees fit. This was the situation that occurred on my watch as a parent and I could not stop it. Now I had to intervene.

Since both of these children were under the age of four, I could not launch into a sermon quoting the appropriate Scriptures about the origin of their sinful nature. I would have liked to have said,

---

[7] At age 0, sing praises to the Lord while holding your baby. Read the Bible out loud so that your infant hears it. Let the peace of God that rules your heart be experienced with your child.

"Listen, children," Psalm 51:5 says: **'Behold, I was brought forth in iniquity, and in sin did my mother conceive me.'** Therefore, you must understand that the two of you have sin natures, so you naturally desire to please yourself whether it pleases God or not. Though God originally created man in His image, now we are born with an image that is marred because of sin. Genesis 5:3 reads: **'When Adam had lived 130 years, he fathered a son in his own likeness** (Adam's), **after his image** (Adam's), **and named him Seth.'** And in Romans 3:23 we read **'for all have sinned and fall short of the glory of God'** and you both have just proven this statement true. In fact, I would go so far as to say that you have proven Ecclesiastes 7:20 true, also: **'For there is not a just man on earth who does good and does not sin.'** Your sinful nature is going to plague you until the Lord saves you **'by grace through faith in Christ Jesus'** (Ephesians. 2:8-9)."

Can you imagine how lost these little ones would be if I sermonized them with all of the above? Not only would they be unable to understand the words and concepts, they would likely tune me out with their short little attention spans. While all of these verses were connected to the explanation of the event, and they are the truth of God's Word, my duty as a parent was to convey these truths to my children in a loving manner on their level—without necessarily quoting chapter and verse! In other words, this event did not occur for me to show off how theologically sound I was compared to them, nor was it about me. This moment was an opportunity to convey these deep truths of God in a simplistic way for the glory of God and the benefit of my children.

Here is how I responded: Consoling the one who got whacked, I held the crying child but spoke to the self-righteous offender first: "I know your sister was selfish by trying to take your toy but you were sinful to hit her." I said it in a calm yet firm voice with eye contact maintained the entire time. "When your sister calms down, you need to make this right. You must repent and ask for forgiveness." The words "repent" and "forgiveness" had already been introduced to them in family devotional times as I presented the Gospel to them at very early ages.

In a situation like this it would seem obvious that the toy was the problem and the solution would be to bring out another toy as a distraction in an attempt to keep everyone happy. In fact, that is what modern day parenting books suggest. But that would be missing the opportunity to teach my children a valuable biblical principle.

The problem was the sin in the heart of my outwardly beautiful child that I loved so dearly. The problem was that he needed to see his heart of sin and his real need for a Savior. Therefore I said: "I want you to pray with me right now and ask Jesus to forgive you of your sin toward your sister." I then led him in a prayer saying, "Lord Jesus, will you forgive my sinful thoughts and actions toward (name inserted)? God, help me to be less selfish and more loving in the future. Amen." The child repeated the prayer after me. Then, I had the child ask forgiveness from the hurting, younger sibling.

As you can imagine, this episode took some time. I was delayed from being able to go back to what I was doing prior to the incident. I took the toy from the older child and placed it on top of the refrigerator. During all of this, the younger child settled down, and was crying softly. I turned to her and said, "If you want to play with a toy that someone else is playing with, you do not try to take it away. You ask the person holding the toy if you can play with it. Or you ask Daddy to help you." I wanted her to know her responsibility in the conflict because they had both sinned.

The Bible tells us that fights and wars come from conflict of desires (James 4:1, 2). Playing with that toy became the desire of my daughter's heart so she took it from her brother. There are two biblical principles apparent in a sibling conflict like this. The desires of our heart motivate us to sin. Know and recognize this. It is not just evil desires that cause us to sin. At the root of the problem is our heart. It is always the heart.

The second principle is that evil can be overcome with good. This is when I taught both children Romans 12:21: **"Do not be overcome with evil, but overcome evil with good."** After quoting the verse, I said, "According to the Bible there is never an excuse to sin. When someone is sinning against us, we are not to be overcome by it or to sin. We are to overcome their sin with good. In other words, you are to be kind to your sibling even when they are unkind to you. It is sinful and wrong to take his toy and it is sinful and wrong to hit your sister with the toy."

Now you might be thinking: "How in the world are children going to understand these big concepts about sin, evil, overcoming, and good?" You might be surprised to know that children are much more teachable than you think. They may not absorb it all, but they are learning and listening more than we know. Your children will learn by their impressions of what they observe in your life and by the repetition of your actions. Because of this, I planned to use this verse again in the future. Your primary goal is to parent the child in a manner that is pleasing to God. When we parent for His glory, we can leave the results up to Him.

We must parent and teach biblical principles at the level of the child's understanding. It helps to have introduced some of the words and concepts to the child prior to the conflict. Introducing new concepts during a conflict is not always the most productive, but sometimes you cannot avoid it. Because of their sinful natures, this was not the only time a problem occurred between these two siblings. My wife and I had to parent them with this same verse quite frequently over the years. If you were to ask either child today about Romans 12:21, they would certainly quote it for you. Further, it is likely that if you ask them to apply this verse appropriately to a real life situation, they will have the ability to do so because of the time and effort invested in training them.

The majority of Christian parents fail to share the Gospel with their children, especially in these teachable moments when the Gospel is clearly needed—such as when a child hits his sibling in the head with a toy. I have discovered that very young children acknowledge the presence and love of God when parents encourage it, especially in the events of everyday life. If God is only mentioned at church on Sundays, do not expect your children to think about Him on the other days of the week. Remind them that the Lord Jesus Christ is a part of each event that occurs in their life. Remind them that they are sinners in need of God's saving grace for justification—which is the Gospel message. When your children become Christians, trusting in Jesus Christ alone for eternal life, remind them that they are *redeemed sinners* who are still in need of God's grace for sanctification, or spiritual growth.

Start the Great Commission in Your Home

Matthew 28:18-20 is commonly called "The Great Commission," as it states: **"And Jesus came and said to them, 'All authority in heaven and on earth has been given to me. Go therefore and make disciples of all nations, baptizing them in the name of the Father and of the Son and of the Holy Spirit, teaching them to observe all**

that I have commanded you. And behold, I am with you always, to the end of the age.'" For our purposes in this book, I want to strongly urge you to be "great commission-minded" in your own home first.

The key words I want to emphasize in this charge from Jesus to the church are to **"go therefore and make disciples...teaching them to observe all that I have commanded you."** This is the primary business of the church: to make disciples—or followers—of Christ. This is the business of your home: to make followers of Christ and to teach them to observe and obey all of His commands. You are simply a steward of your children and not their owner. You control the structure of their lives in the role of a parent; however, ultimate control and authority belongs to the Lord. They are His children first and yours second.

God has placed these children in your life for His purposes. He wants you to disciple them. "Disciple" is the root word of discipline and that is precisely how Jesus trained His twelve disciples. He taught and disciplined them as their rabbi, or teacher. Matthew 28:18-20 is your commission from Jesus to teach and disciple your children as stated in verse 18: **"All authority in heaven and on earth has been given to Me."**

You could think of the command to make disciples as a "co-mission," reminding yourself that it involves two persons: Jesus Christ and you. It is a work of the Holy Spirit (Christ) and parents. You are partnering with Christ to fulfill His mission for the children He has given you for a season of life. You should desire that your children be committed followers and disciples of Christ and not just followers of you as a parent.

In His great commission, verse 19 uses the word "go," which could be translated "as you are going." In other words, "As you are going therefore, make disciples," meaning that wherever you go in whatever activity or way the Lord leads you in your everyday life, make disciples of Christ. Build relationships with others and point them to Christ. This is not an option. God expects you to fulfill this command for His glory and as you do, He will lead you. In essence, as you go forth and live your lives, you are to make disciples of your children and anyone else God brings across your paths.

Your children need to spend time with you on a daily basis. I am a proponent of quantity time, and do not accept the excuse that quality time is just as important as quantity of time. When there is quantity of time spent with a child, there is usually quality involved, but it must be intentional for this to be true. How much of an influence are you in your child's life? How much television does your child watch each day? In his book, *Everyday Talk*, John Younts writes that American children spend an average of 35 minutes per week talking to their fathers. This statistic breaks down to only 5 minutes each day![8] How much intentional discipleship can take place when a father is spending merely five minutes each day with his child? The obvious answer is not very much.

Contrast this brief amount of quality time with the statistics that the average teenager spends three hours each day watching television, and the average preschooler watches TV four hours each day.[9] Which is having a greater influence upon the child? The twenty-one to twenty-eight hours each week spent watching the worldly messages of television or the thirty-five minutes the child spends talking to Dad? Do you spend time with your child, or does the world influence his thinking? Is your television "babysitting" your preschooler or are you intentionally teaching him about Jesus and His Word?

Quite naturally, children have a precious faith. Jesus Christ even taught His followers to have the "faith of a child" in Mark 10:15: **"Truly, I say to you, whoever does not receive the kingdom of God like a child shall not enter it."** How is a child's faith different from an adult's faith? It is simply that children will believe almost anything they are told. Some would call it "gullible," but it is a precious gift of God to believe others. Children especially believe those they spend the most time with and will believe television shows, ungodly peer influences, ungodly teachers, and the like. Your child is learning to trust the things he watches and hears on television if the majority of his time is spent in that activity each week. Limit the influence of television upon your children today and instead encourage them to read a good book.[10]

Children are by nature imitators. They watch and learn and listen. If you live your life as an imitator of Jesus Christ, your children will see that as good. 3 John 11 teaches, **"Beloved, do not imitate evil but**

---

[8] Younts, John A. *Everyday Talk*, Shepherd Press, Wapwallopen, PA, p. 16.
[9] Ibid, p. 19.
[10] Be careful with some library books that seem harmless on the outside but teach worldly concepts that oppose the Word of God.

imitate good. **Whoever does good is from God; whoever does evil has not seen God."** Be intentional about protecting your child from the evil influences of TV, internet, and bad company.

Children will be also influenced by their peers and it will likely bring them down according to 1 Corinthians 15:33, **"Do not be deceived: 'Bad company ruins good morals.'"** The Lord warns us not to deceive ourselves into thinking we will bring bad company up to His moral standards. In fact, it is just the opposite: their bad company will ruin our good moral standards.

When parents hope that their children will be "salt and light" for a public school world full of unbelievers, they are often not thinking biblically. Bible application would demonstrate that the most likely outcome is that children who are raised in a Christian home but spend most of their day with worldly influences, including peers at school, teachers who do not think God is real, and television that promotes ungodliness, will be negatively impacted by the worldly messages they are receiving.

As a parent, your duty is to obey Proverbs 22:6: **"Train up a child in the way he should go; even when he is old he will not depart from it."** Training is primarily concerned with your child's will and the building up of godly habits. Training cultivates the child's heart to possess the correct motivation to glorify God in how he thinks, speaks, and acts. Lessons much of the time consist of lectures and discipline, which are insufficient to produce godliness.

As a parent, be sure you have the right goals in mind. First, teach your child that pleasing God is your top priority and it should be theirs as well. This motivation comes when eternity is in focus and not just the temporal benefits of momentarily pleasing a parent. Place eternity before your child's eyes as often as you have the opportunity. Bring God into the little moments in his life. Demonstrate to your children the grace God has given you. Your first goal must be to glorify God.

Your second goal must be to help your child to become more like Christ in thought, word, and deed. Make the most of the time you are given by teaching him about Christ and biblical principles in everyday life. If you will keep these two goals in the forefront of your thinking, you will be doing a successful job of parenting. Be the best parent you can be, but focus more on your effort to please God than your own abilities during the process of parenting. Then, let God be concerned with the outcome He desires for His own glory.

Conclusion

The encouraging aspect of making disciples of Christ is that God does not expect you to do it alone or in your own strength. The final verse of this Great Commission states: **"And behold, I am with you always, even to the end of the age."** Point your children to Christ at every opportunity. Pray that God will call them to be His disciples and that they will respond. Your goal is to teach them to obey the Holy Scriptures and commandments of God and instruct them in the Christian faith.

Your job as a parent is not simply to change the apparent behavior of your child. Your mission is to let Christ change the inner heart of your child, which includes attitudes, thoughts, emotions, and motives. Real heart change will lead to external behavior changes and you are not powerful enough to change your child's heart. Only Christ can do that, and He does so through your parental instructions that agree with His Word. Christ works through parents to teach children and to turn their hearts to Him.

KEY IDEAS AND PRACTICAL THINGS TO DO

1. Take thirty minutes each day to read and discuss the Bible with your child.

2. Share the Gospel with your child. Be sure to include your need and your child's need for a Savior due to sin.

3. Teach your child to pray to God by modeling your prayer life before your child. Spend a short time of prayer with your child each day asking God for the grace needed to glorify Him, do His will, and to become more like Christ. Model the Lord's Prayer given in Matthew 6:9-15.

Chapter 3
Who is Responsible?

When Derrick gets home after football practice, he quickly unloads his backpack in his bedroom and begins rolling several cigarettes with the marijuana he bought from Scott. His mother yells, "Derrick, dinner is ready. Come, eat." Derrick doesn't respond and continues making "joints" to take with him to the big party tonight. Fifteen minutes later, Derrick's mother bursts into his room with one earring in her hand and the other in her ear saying, "Derrick, go eat before the food gets any colder." She notices the rolling papers and drugs and says, "Derrick, you better get rid of that stuff by the time I get back from my date tonight! I'm leaving now—my boyfriend's here." She turns and rushes out of his room and out of the front door.

The Ten Commandments (Exodus 20) are well known even to non-Christians and are often misunderstood to be a list of "do not's" given by God to "spoil our fun" as human beings. However, nothing could be further from the truth. The Ten Commandments must be viewed through the eyes of God's great love for us; He knows our limitations and what choices will harm us. God wants us to have the right kind of pleasure, which involves having a right relationship with Him and with other people.

In the Ten Commandments, the first four commandments address mankind's relationship with God (Exodus 20:3-11). Problems with "addiction" involve a violation of the first commandment: **"You shall have no other gods before Me"** (Exodus 20:3). When Christians get their relationship with Christ out of its proper order and substitute a desire for any substance or material thing more than they desire to be in God's will, they are breaking this commandment.

While the first four commandments deal with man's relationship with God, the final six commandments address man's relationships with others (Exodus 20:12-17). It is interesting to note that the very first of the relational commandments is centered upon the family unit; the family is of primary importance to God and it is vital that we learn how to properly interact within our family structure. **"Honor your father and your mother that your days may be long in the land that the LORD your God is giving you"** (Exodus 20:12). This verse is also the first commandment with a promise—the promise of a long life—which is something most everyone aspires to possess!

But who is this commandment addressed to? If you answer "everyone," you are right, but look a little closer. Who specifically is supposed to obey this commandment in order to receive the promise? This commandment is specifically addressing *children* who are told to honor their parents! If you are a parent, then this truth should free you from taking responsibility in areas where your child is really responsible.

Your child is ultimately responsible for his choices of "addiction." No matter how poor your parenting skills were, no matter how tough the environment was for your child, no matter what genetic make-up is in your child from parental DNA, he is ultimately responsible to obey both the first and fifth commandments for his own benefit. Your child is responsible before the Lord. This truth will be explored in more detail later in this book but I do hope it encourages you now.

The Importance of the Family Unit

Children must honor their parents' God-given authority in the home.[11] If a child does not learn to submit, obey, and respect his parents at home, he will assuredly fail to submit to other authorities in his life such as teachers, police officers, and the like. If house rules are violated through willful disobedience, then most assuredly society's laws will be violated through willful disobedience.

Children have been given parents as a blessing by God for the purpose of providing protection, discipline, instruction, and spiritual nourishment. Children must learn submission to authority in the home. Therefore, they are to honor their parents as unto the Lord and are commanded not to rebel against them. In drug abuse and addiction situations, a child is almost always dishonoring and disobeying a parent's commands. It is simply rebellion in the child's heart; he or she is thinking, "I know better than my parents," even though God has placed the parent as the authority over that child.

One of Satan's primary tricks is to convince us that God's authority is not good. Even further, God's choice of human authorities—like imperfect parents—cannot be good either, according to Satan's logic.

---

[11] Some children are raised by grandparents or other guardians. The principle remains the same that the child must learn to obey those who are in the parental role to the child.

In Genesis 3:1-5, the Bible clearly shows us Satan's game plan in the first event of disobedience, disrespect, and dishonor to God and His Word:

> **Now the serpent was more crafty than any other beast of the field that the LORD God had made. He said to the woman, "Did God actually say, 'You shall not eat of any tree in the garden'" And the woman said to the serpent, "We may eat of the fruit of the trees in the garden, but God said, 'You shall not eat of the fruit of the tree that is in the midst of the garden, neither shall you touch it, lest you die.'" But the serpent said to the woman, "You will not surely die. For God knows that when you eat of it your eyes will be opened, and you will be like God, knowing good and evil.'"**

In this passage Satan asks the first question in history designed to plant a seed of doubt about God, His Word, and His authority. Satan appeals to Eve by promising her that she "will be like God." Eve was already "like God" in the sense that she was made in His image. But in Satan's crafty plan, he is stating that Adam and Eve do not need to submit to God or to trust His Word because they can be their own gods. Even today, Satan wants us to believe that God's authority is not legitimate and that we can know what is best for us. He whispers, "You don't need to submit to God's authority because you cannot trust God at His Word. Besides, you know just as much as God does anyway." This is the multi-layered lie that Satan would have you believe about our holy, loving Father God. You must not believe his lies but rather trust the inerrant, sufficient truth of the Holy Scriptures, which are God's inspired Word (2 Timothy 3:16-17). Scripture commands us to trust and obey God as we first trust and obey our human parents and authorities.

Can you see how those same old lies of Satan can be manifested in the heart and mind of a rebellious child? The sad reality is that our sinful hearts still want us to be our own god, unwilling to yield to any higher authority. That is why the fifth commandment to children is so important.

Do you understand the significance of this biblical principle? Your children are commanded by God to honor you, the parent, which will lead to a special promise by God of a life of longevity. In other places in the Bible, there are commands given to parents to raise their children in a godly manner (Genesis 18:19; Psalm 78:4; Ephesians 6:4; and Deuteronomy 6:7: **"You shall teach them** (my words) **diligently to your children, and shall talk of them when you sit in your house, and when you walk by the way, and when you lie down, and when you rise"** (Explanation mine). Parents are not to be irresponsible in their duties, yet this fifth command is the responsibility of the child to honor the parents that God has placed in authority over them. Despite the best parenting in the world, some children disobey this commandment and must learn life lessons the hard way.

Be sure to grasp the importance of this biblical truth. God gave us Ten Commandments designed to help us know that His ways are the best way to live and one of them specifically addresses your children and the importance of obedience! If your children cannot read, they will need your help in learning this great principle of obedience. Teach this great principle to your child at an early age. Utilize it frequently in your addiction-proof parenting. Point your children to Christ by helping them see that their thoughts, words, and actions toward you as their parent are connected to their heart toward God.

In the Beginning

When children are born, they need no training in selfishness. A baby cries when he is hungry, when his diaper is wet or dirty, and when he's sleepy. A child is never taught to throw a temper tantrum when he does not get his way. Children do not need instructions in how to rebel against authorities. This is not learned behavior. Children simply are hardwired with this selfish, sinful nature, and have been ever since mankind's sin in Genesis 3.

Left alone, a child will inherently gravitate toward pleasing his own fleshly desires for pleasure and the avoidance of pain. All on his own he will choose to please himself over pleasing God. It is the inevitable curse of sin. There is nothing learned about these behaviors and thought patterns. A tough environment does not cause a child to become selfish. It is in his sinful nature and it is reinforced by sinful choices daily.

Therefore, parents are responsible to teach their child about Christ and His Word so that he can be saved by the power of the

Holy Spirit. He needs a new nature to replace the old nature. Romans 10:14-15a states: **"But how are they to call on him in whom they have not believed? And how are they to believe in him of whom they have never heard? And how are they to hear without someone preaching? And how are they to preach unless they are sent?"** Children need to hear the Gospel at home and at church because they do not start in neutral when they are born. They do not have a clean slate as some psychologists would have you believe. Instead, children are born with a nature that will lead them to destruction both physically and spiritually. Without divine intervention and faithful discipline and instruction using the Scriptures, children will not be saved.

This is why the Word of God is so important. Children need to learn the truth of God's Word because it reveals Jesus Christ to us, and that reveals God's character to us. Without the truth of God's Word, we will not come to the supernatural understanding that God is good, holy, and perfect. This world is cursed by mankind's sin (Genesis 3). When I look around, I often see hurt, heartache, sin, death, greed, lust, drunkenness, idolatry, murder, and all sorts of evil. Very often, I do not see purity, which is where God is most clearly seen—in Christ. Matthew 5:8 states: **"Blessed are the pure in heart, for they shall see God."** You and your child will learn best about God from the Bible.

Left alone without instruction from the truth of the Holy Scriptures, your child will not see God in the circumstances of everyday life. It is a sobering thought. This is why the Gospel message of the Bible is essential to salvation. 1 Corinthians 1:18 reminds us: **"For the word of the cross is folly to those who are perishing, but to us who are being saved it is the power of God."** The only source of this salvation message is the Holy Bible shared verbally and in practice by God's faithful servants.

As a parent, your job is to teach this fifth commandment to your child at a very young age. Teach your child to trust you and to see your authority as good. When I am involved in biblical counseling sessions with rebellious persons, one verse I utilize frequently is 1 Peter 2:18: **"Servants, be subject to your masters with all respect, not only to the good and gentle but also to the unjust."** Though not specifically a verse addressed to children, this biblical principle of respecting an "unjust" and unfair authority figure is a powerful lesson.

Parents are not perfect, yet a child must honor them even when the imperfect parent seems unfair. Any human authority that God places over us will *not* be perfect. However, perfection is not what God requires. God requires people in authority to serve the best interests of those He has placed under their care. Likewise, God requires people under authority to honor those He has *sovereignly* chosen to lead because it is ultimately an act of trusting God. It is an act of faith to submit to an imperfect authority figure. By submitting to imperfect, God-given authorities, one is trusting God, who has the king's heart in His sovereign Hands according to Proverbs 21:1: **"The king's heart is a stream of water in the hand of the LORD; he turns it wherever he will."**

Parents need help. Where does this help come from? The answer is the Holy Spirit. Parents need the Holy Spirit to empower them to do God's will (Philippians 2:12-13). Children need the Holy Spirit to remove their heart of stone and replace it with the Holy Spirit. The Word of God and the Holy Spirit always work together according to Ephesians 6:17, which calls the Word **"the sword of the Spirit."** Reading, studying, and memorizing the Word of God is essential because the Holy Spirit uses the Word to teach and direct us. Imagine trying to bake a cake without eggs, water, and oil. Those ingredients are essential to baking a cake. Likewise, the Word of God is an essential ingredient for salvation AND spiritual growth (called sanctification). The Word of God provides the Holy Spirit with the proper ingredients inside of a person to bring godly change and strengthened faith.

Conclusion

As we go forward to understand and learn addiction-proof parenting we must remember that we are not perfect people who perfectly follow God's commands. Addiction-proof parenting involves parents who are willing to submit themselves to Christ and to teach this principle to their children who are their God-given disciples. A wife and mother who submits to her husband as unto the Lord (Ephesians 5:22) will model submission to authority before her children. A wife's submission is a key element since children learn more from what parents do than what they say to do. A husband or father who submits to the laws of the land as unto the Lord will model submission to authority to his children. In other words, do not speed when driving your car, Dad!

Ultimately, your children are held responsible by the Lord to obey the first and fifth commandments just as parents were responsible to obey these commandments when they were children and are now as adults. How well did you honor your father and/or mother when you were growing up? Do you need to ask their forgiveness? Is God humbling you through your children now? I frequently say to my wife, "There is nothing like parenting to humble us before the Lord." Pray that the Lord will teach you to trust in Him and the lessons He is teaching you, as you parent children who are stubborn, selfish, and self-centered from birth and in need of much discipline.

KEY IDEAS AND PRACTICAL THINGS TO DO

1. Read the fifth commandment to your child and talk about its meaning at length. Use practical examples in your own life of when you obeyed and disobeyed this commandment along with the blessings (or not) that followed.

2. Read the first commandment to your child and talk about its meaning at length. Use practical examples in your life and your child's that demonstrate how easily we all are tempted to serve other idols for our own selfish gain. For example, maybe your child loves a toy, video game, or the like more than he/she loves to spend time serving others, reading the Bible, or praying. Examples are not difficult to find.

3. Play the Obedience Game with your child. Give your child a command to do (i.e. put your shoes in your closet) and then commend your child for obedience. Though you want to be serious at first, feel free to laugh and have some fun doing this exercise after awhile. Get your child to practice obeying your commands.

Chapter 4
Discipline in Love

Derrick arrives at Freddie's house. He is the star football player and this is his eighteenth birthday party. Derrick sees his friend, Raymond, getting out of his car with four girls he drove to the party. "Hey, Raymond," Derrick whispers, "I brought some good stuff I got from Scott for us—for later." They go inside at the same time as someone excitedly announces, "The keg is in the backyard, Guys!" The drinking begins at Freddie's house while his parents are away at the lake for the weekend.

Imagine a school classroom with no discipline and twenty-five children who all have a sinful nature and a desire to please themselves above all else. Can you see the paper airplanes flying through the air and most of the students talking or text messaging each other on their cell phones? How much learning occurs in this undisciplined, unstructured, and unloving environment?

Discipline is essential for classroom education, and it is just as necessary in the home. Most people react negatively to the word "discipline" because they have either been disciplined in sinful anger or never at all. Both extremes have damaging effects upon a child and can contribute to "addictive thinking" and must be avoided.

The first extreme is discipline in anger. If you have ever been disciplined in sinful anger, it is likely that you received yelling, physical abuse, and excessive emotional pain. This type of discipline is wrong, unproductive, and sinful. It is not biblical discipline administered in love. It contributes to defeated, hopeless attitudes in a child and a desire to escape from the extreme pain in any way possible. Sinful discipline can contribute to an apathetic attitude in the child who then develops an "I don't care" way of thinking.

Equally damaging is the second extreme—neglecting to discipline a child in love. In many ways, this extreme may have worse consequences than disciplining in sinful anger. Many people who struggle with various addictions are undisciplined. They grow up without authority figures, learn to trust themselves, and learn to make decisions without any input from others. They live as though they are independent and no one else exists in this world. They distrust others who disagree with them, especially authority figures.

There are many more complications from neglecting to discipline a child in love that will be revealed later in this book.

Take a moment to assess your parenting style. Which extreme most characterizes your tendency in parenting: excessive anger or neglecting to discipline at all? Does your spouse tend to err on the opposite extreme? Many parents differ in this tendency, which becomes the source of conflict regarding the discipline of their children. To be honest, my wife and I fall on both sides of the ditch and usually opposite from each other. Parents must learn to be balanced in a biblical approach to discipline.

Biblical and addiction-proof parenting is balanced when the truth is presented to the child in the love of Christ (Ephesians 4:15). The child needs to know the truth, since it is the truth that sets us free (John 8:32), and needs to be reassured of your love and God's love, since God is love (1 John 4:8). Christians grow spiritually to become more like Christ when the truth in love is spoken to them by other believers in the body of Christ, according to Ephesians 4:15-16: **"Rather, speaking the truth in love, we are to grow up in every way into him who is the head, into Christ, from whom the whole body, joined and held together by every joint with which it is equipped, when each part is working properly, makes the body grow so that it builds itself up in love."** A child's spiritual growth hinges upon learning the truth of God's Word in the love of the Holy Spirit. Wrap the truth in love when you discipline and teach your child and it will yield much fruit.

Perfection is Not the Goal

Your children are your God-given disciples. Just as Jesus' twelve disciples lived with Him, your disciples live with you, and you are to disciple your children in the same way. Did He preach a verbal sermon to these twelve men every day? Not likely! He lived His life in a transparent way before them so they could watch Him interact with others in His perfect compassion. They learned to model Jesus and to think like He did. Jesus taught them in the everyday moments of life. He corrected and rebuked when necessary and He encouraged them always. He maximized the teachable moments in the disciples' lives by building a gracious learning environment where they were free to fail and then learn from those failures.

In Matthew 6:31-33, Jesus gave them the following encouragement. He said, **"Therefore, do not be anxious, saying, 'What shall we eat?' or 'What shall we drink?' or 'What shall we wear?' For the Gentiles seek after all these things, and your heavenly Father knows that you need them. But seek first the kingdom of God and His righteousness, and all these things will be added to you."** Later, in Matthew 8:26, He gently rebuked the disciples when they came to him in fear, **"And he said to them, 'Why are you afraid, O you of little faith?'"**

Let this give you hope. None of us are Jesus. None of us are perfect parents. Even Jesus experienced the heartache of one of His disciples betraying Him and choosing to disobey God. Judas Iscariot lived, walked, and ate with Jesus, yet Judas missed it. When I think about Judas, I wonder how he could make such horrible choices when he was as close to Jesus as anyone. Like Judas, your children may also choose to disobey God and betray the example you have set for them. They are responsible for their sinful choices. As a parent, you are responsible for training them in the discipline and admonition of the Lord (Ephesians 6:4), but you cannot control their choices.

I believe one reason that Judas' betrayal is recorded is to give parents hope. Unlike Jesus in His perfection, we will fail and sin against our children when we are angry. When we do so, we must confess our sins to God and to our children. Then, we must forsake (or repent of) our sins according to Proverbs 28:13: **"Whoever conceals his transgressions will not prosper, but he who confesses and forsakes them will obtain mercy."** Christians are not perfect people who never sin. Therefore, when we sin, we must model the Christian response which is brokenness over our sin, asking for forgiveness from God and from those we have hurt. We must also model repentance—meaning we think, speak, and act differently, in accordance with God's Word.

I urge you not to think that you must be perfect before your children. You are setting yourself up for failure if your goal is to be perfect. It will not happen. We are to be role models, but what that means is that we model repentance and forgiveness when we "blow it" in front of our children. Doing so is reflective of the Gospel of grace.

What is Discipline?

In Ephesians 6:4b, Paul gives this directive to parents: **"bring them up in the discipline and instruction of the Lord."** Parents who desire to follow this command may have difficulty discerning God's definition of "discipline." Certainly it is a controversial term in our culture today.

Though they sometimes resemble each other, "discipline" and "punishment" are different terms. Punishment is the infliction of a penalty for wrongdoing. In His justice, God had to punish the sins of mankind. He could not "wink" at sin by letting it go unpunished. Sin came into the world by one man (Adam) according to 1 Corinthians 15:21-22: **"For as by a man came death, by a man has come also the resurrection of the dead. For as in Adam all die, so also in Christ shall all be made alive."** The good news is that by one man (Jesus) all of mankind can be saved because the Lord punished the sins of mankind through Jesus' death on the cross. Let's being by defining what discipline is *not*:

Discipline is not punishment. Discipline is defined as "training that corrects, molds, or perfects the mental faculties or moral character."[12] Biblically, it is training with a purpose. Disciples are under the discipline of their teacher. Disciples of Christ are under the discipline of Christ. All Christians are disciples of Christ by the work of the Holy Spirit as they are being trained, taught, sanctified, molded, and perfected into the "mental faculties and moral character" of Jesus Christ. Christians are to become like Christ in thoughts, words, and actions.

Discipline may mean that a child cannot always do what he wants to do. It may not always be fun but it will be beneficial to him long-term. Children need discipline. They need restrictions. Little children and young people who have not been disciplined in love often tend to view their experiences as punishment. Most often, it has been harsh. In the chapters ahead, as we study the factors that contribute to addictive behavior, we will see that discipline— imposed by parents, teachers or self has a great impact on a child's spiritual growth.

Discipline is not condemnation. Romans 8:1 is a verse very precious to Christians: **"There is therefore now no condemnation**

---

[12] Merriam-Webster, Inc. *Merriam-Webster's Collegiate Dictionary.* Includes Index. 10th ed. Springfield, Mass., U.S.A.: Merriam-Webster, 1996, c1993.

for those who are in Christ Jesus." Read the rest of Romans 8 and you will see the contrast between walking in the flesh and walking in the Holy Spirit. Condemnation is for unbelievers whose minds are set upon the flesh and the temporary pleasures of this world. According to God's Word, those persons will spend an eternity in hell if they fail to repent and trust in Christ Jesus for eternal life.

Believers continue to struggle with the internal presence of sin that battles against the indwelling of the Holy Spirit. The Holy Spirit brings "conviction" to us as children of God that is designed to change our thoughts, words, and actions. Conviction may be painful for a season but it is painful for a reason. Our heavenly Father wants us to submit to Him and when we do not, He corrects us for our own good and for His own purposes. He alone is a perfect Father who can be trusted to determine the appropriate discipline. Use the word "discipline" rather than "punishment" when you deal with your child. Use the word "discipleship" for what you and others will be doing to help your child become Christ-like. Remember Hebrews 12:5-11 states:

> **And have you forgotten the exhortation that addresses you as sons? "My son, do not regard lightly the discipline of the Lord, nor be weary when reproved by him. For the Lord disciplines the one he loves, and chastises every son whom he receives. It is for discipline that you have to endure. God is treating you as sons. For what son is there whom his father does not discipline? If you are left without discipline, in which all have participated, then you are illegitimate children and not sons. Besides this, we have had earthly fathers who disciplined us and we respected them. Shall we not much more be subject to the Father of spirits and live? For they disciplined us for a short time as it seemed best to them, but he disciplines us for our good, that we may share his holiness. For the moment all discipline seems painful rather than pleasant, but later it yields the peaceful fruit of righteousness to those who have been trained by it."**

Discipline is not wrath. The reason that discipline is not wrath is that believers in Christ receive "no condemnation" from God for they are "in Christ Jesus." Christ Jesus received the wrath of God and punishment for our sins on the cross at Calvary. God's wrath was fully satisfied in that event and Jesus said: "It is finished," meaning the debt was paid in full. Because Jesus took on the wrath of God for our sins, we must never administer our wrath on our child. We must put away all wrath and malice in dealing with our children (Colossians 3) and put on love. We received only grace from God and that is what we must show our children. (More on this topic in Ch. 7). Being "born again" gives us the power to overcome the flesh and its sinful tendencies. We have the ability to say "no" to the desires of our flesh and to say "yes" to the Holy Spirit's leading to obedience to His Word. Christians can choose to obey God and not sin.

Conclusion

God disciplines us because He loves us. God wants "good" for us and He alone knows what best motivates His children to obey Him. Obeying Him is the best way for a child of God to live, and to disobey is sinful and brings heartache. Hebrews 12:11 reminds us that discipline seems painful and unpleasant for a moment. When people are obedient to the Lord, the Lord is pleased. When children are obedient to their parents who love them and want good for them, parents are pleased as well as the Lord. When children obey their parents who discipline them in the love of the Lord (Ephesians 6:4), they are protected, disciplined, trained, and on the way to becoming "addiction-proof."

KEY IDEAS AND PRACTICAL THINGS TO DO

1. Play the Obedience Game again. This time ask your child to cover his/her ears when you give a command which emphasizes the importance of listening.

2. Play the Obedience Game again but this time, have your child play the role of parent and you be the child. Model obedience before your

child. If you are married, get both parents involved.

3. Read the biblical account of Samson (Judges 13-16, Hebrews 11:32) to find an example of how disobedience led to heartache for one of God's children.

Chapter 5
The Rod and Reproof

After drinking for awhile, Derrick and Raymond smoke a marijuana cigarette with some of the other boys in a back bedroom. They laugh and lose track of time while taking turns playing violent video games that belong to Freddie. Popping his head in the room, Freddie says to Derrick and Raymond, "When you guys get done with that game, come out here with me. I want you to meet somebody." Derrick and Raymond quit playing the game and meet Freddie's new friend, Matt, who introduces the boys to a new drug, Adderall.®

Warning: The following chapter is not for the weak in faith or the worldly-minded person. If you are a Christian who reads the Bible infrequently and is heavily influenced by secular ideas, then you will struggle with the principles presented in this chapter. If you are a Christian who loves the grace of God but struggles with the justice of God, then you may not like this chapter. I am reluctant to write this at the beginning of a chapter but I want to warn you and to challenge you to keep reading this book. Do not dismiss the importance of this chapter and the message that the Lord wants to communicate to you in the following pages.

Do you trust God? Most people say, "Yes, of course!" But the reality is that most people *say* they trust God but *act* as though they trust themselves more. God warns us all against this tendency to trust ourselves more than God in Proverbs 3:5-8: **"Trust in the LORD with all your heart, and do not lean on your own understanding. In all your ways acknowledge him, and he will make straight your paths. Be not wise in your own eyes; fear the LORD, and turn away from evil. It will be healing to your flesh and refreshment to your bones."** I urge you to trust God more than you trust your own feelings and beliefs if they do not align with God's Word. Reading this chapter may challenge your faith and trust in God.

Trusting the Lord is central to implementing the fundamentals of this chapter. It may be challenging to apply loving discipline to your child in the form of the rod and reproof. The rod is physical discipline and reproof is verbal discipline and instruction. Both are necessary to addiction-proof your child. I know from personal experience how difficult it can be, but I would simply point you to what God says in His Word.

God's Word is to be acted upon in obedience and trust in the Lord. The Bible is inspired by God (2 Timothy 3:16) meaning it is authored by Him. The words are His words, recorded by men, and written through them. The Bible can be misinterpreted just as any communication can be misunderstood by the receiver. God's Word is perfect and we have to understand that misinterpreting and misunderstanding it is therefore our problem, not His. We can only understand His Word by the power of the Holy Spirit.

Do you trust God's Word? Let's see if you do. Here are some excerpts about discipline, wisdom, the rod, and reproof from the book of Proverbs:

- **"My son, do not despise the LORD's discipline or be weary of his reproof, for the LORD reproves him whom he loves, as a father the son in whom he delights"** (Proverbs 3:11-12).
- **"Whoever spares the rod hates his son, but he who loves him is diligent to discipline him"** (Proverbs 13:24).
- **"Folly is bound up in the heart of a child, but the rod of discipline drives it far from him"** (Proverbs 22:15).
- **"Do not withhold discipline from a child; if you strike him with a rod, he will not die"** (Proverbs 23:13).
- **"If you strike him with the rod, you will save his soul from Sheol"** (Proverbs 23:14). ("Sheol" literally means "the grave" which is physical death).
- **"The rod and reproof give wisdom, but a child left to himself brings shame to his mother. Discipline your son, and he will give you rest; he will give delight to your heart"** (Proverbs 29:15, 17).

Before we look at each of these verses, let me repeat that you must trust the Lord and His Word. If you listen to popular psychological opinion, you will likely skip this chapter and fail to implement the principles contained herein. If you do, you will likely see selfish, "addictive thinking" in your child when he grows into adulthood. You may not believe me now, but addiction-proof parenting utilizes the rod and reproof as tools to administer discipline in love for the glory of God.

Trusting the Lord at His Word means that you understand the authority structure that He set up in His divine justice. To the government, God gives the sword to keep the peace and for the good of all mankind (Romans 13:4). To the church, God gives clear church discipline to keep the peace and purity (Matthew18:15-20). To the parents, God gives the rod and reproof of loving discipline to keep the peace and purity of the home (Proverbs 22:15; Proverbs 29:15). Can you see a pattern here? In God's justice, He provides a tool for each of His appointed governing authorities to utilize in order to keep the peace and purity of the entity they govern.

The bottom line is this: if you trust God, then you will learn to administer the rod and reproof in a loving, planned, disciplined, and purposeful manner for the glory of God and for the benefit of your child. Do you really trust God? This is what Tedd Tripp, author of *Shepherding a Child's Heart,* has to say on this subject:

> God has commanded the use of the rod in discipline and correction of children. It is not the only thing you do, but it must be used. He has told you that there are needs within your children that require the use of the rod. If you are going to rescue your children from death, if you are going to root out the folly that is bound up in their hearts, if you are going to impart wisdom, you must use the rod. The rod is a parent, in faith toward God and faithfulness toward his or her children, undertaking the responsibility of careful, timely, measured and controlled use of physical punishment to underscore the importance of obeying God, thus rescuing the child from continuing in his foolishness until death.[13]

---

[13] Tripp, Tedd. *Shepherding a Child's Heart,* Shepherd Press, Wapwallopen, PA, 1995, p.108

What Does God Say?

Proverbs 3:11-12: **"My son, do not despise the LORD's discipline or be weary of his reproof, for the LORD reproves him whom he loves, as a father the son in whom he delights."** Proverbs, chapter three is a very rich chapter. Verses 5-8 were mentioned earlier in this chapter as they encourage us not to lean upon our own understanding but to trust God. Now, verses 11 and 12 remind us of what was covered in the previous chapter: God loves His children and because of His great love, He disciplines and reproves us because He desires for us to gain wisdom and to prosper (verses 13-27). God knows His children will not prosper if they think like the world's system and live an undisciplined lifestyle.

What is a "reproof"? A "reproof" is simply a "criticism for a fault."[14] It is administered by an authority who is expressing disapproval in a gentle manner. In fact, the verb form of reproof is "reprove" which "implies an often kindly intent to correct a fault," according to Webster's dictionary.[15] When we are at fault for wrongdoing, we need criticism to help us change. Notice the words "kindly intent" in the definition of "reprove." Galatians 6:1a states: **"Brothers, if anyone is caught in any transgression, you who are spiritual should restore him in a spirit of gentleness."** A spirit of gentleness is possible whenever you reprove and restore someone caught in sin, but often parents are so angry that they fail to be gentle when correcting their child.

What is your spirit when you discipline your child? While you might not hit or spank your child, do you yell and scream in a spirit of anger and rage? No matter what discipline methods you use, biblical parenting should be discipline in love, which always involves a spirit of gentleness. You may be asking, "How do I spank my child in a spirit of gentleness? Isn't that a contradiction?" No, your attitude toward the discipline of your child is the key. You must plan ahead to gently administer loving discipline for the correction of your child.

Do not be shocked when your children disobey because they have a selfish, sinful nature. You must understand that their misbehavior is a product of their sinful heart and not a personal attack against

---

[14] Merriam-Webster, Inc. *Merriam-Webster's Collegiate Dictionary.* Includes Index. 10th ed. Springfield, Mass., U.S.A.: Merriam-Webster, 1996, c1993.
[15] Ibid.

you. *Likewise, your use of the rod and reproof is not a personal attack against your child.* You are acting out of duty to God and for your child's best long-term interests and the child will not understand this until he matures. Be sure to remind him that his choices have led to this outcome. Put the responsibility upon your child and his choice to obey or disobey.

Some parents do discipline in an extremely angry and abusive manner because they take personal offense at the child's disobedience. These parents make their child's disobedience a conflict between parent and child when it is really a conflict between the child and God. The child's disobedience is a product of his selfish desire to be "god" of his own life. As a parent, you are getting in the way of his desire to be in control. He wants to be the authority in his life and does not appreciate your parental authority or God's ultimate authority. Therefore, he disobeys, often wanting to find out who really is the boss.

Biblical Application of the Rod and Reproof

The Bible commands and encourages parents to utilize the rod AND reproof because it is balanced according to Proverbs 29:15: **"The rod and reproof give wisdom, but a child left to himself brings shame to his mother."** The rod is physical discipline while the reproof is the verbal correction. Physical discipline is best coupled with a verbal reproof for balanced discipline.

Again, some parents err by using the rod without a reproof while other parents err by providing reproofs without a rod. One extreme is too harsh (rod but no reproof) and the other extreme is too soft (reproof but no rod). Both extremes are less effective than a balanced approach combining the rod and reproof. Your child needs physical correction and verbal correction.

For those who are afraid that the rod is cruel, let me carefully and biblically define the use of the rod for you. When I refer to the rod in this book, I am referring to a thin wooden instrument like a switch, dowel, or paint mixing stick. Let me explain. The Bible clearly endorses the use of the rod and NOT the hand for spankings. Some parents think "popping their child on the mouth" is more acceptable than using a small dowel that can be purchased from the local store. Some parents think that "slapping their child with their hand" is more humane than using a switch or thin tree branch for spanking. Hitting your child with your hand is *not* endorsed by the Scriptures; many times this even qualifies as child abuse.

Why does the Bible *not* say to hit your child with your hand? One reason may be that hand hitting has the potential for making you more susceptible to being led by your emotions. When a parent is extremely angry, correction can easily get out of control and be excessive. Some parents who do not spank get so angry with their children's lack of discipline that they finally explode in anger and yell at or hit their child. God does not consider this appropriate discipline. It is sinful. In fact, Jesus said that if you have gotten to this point of anger then you have murdered in your heart already.

The Lord wants parents to be under control when they correct their children. Parents are wise to have a small, thin instrument that is dedicated to the function of administering physical discipline. In fact, having to go retrieve this instrument from its place of storage slows a parent down, allows him time to collect his thoughts, and bring more purposeful teaching to the moment. Parents must always plan ahead and not react out of emotion. The rod must be administered with purpose: correcting the child's behavior and teaching the child that disobedient choices lead to painful consequences. For example, the momentary consequences of a rod are far less painful than running into traffic and getting hit by a car. Also, the rod is far less painful than dealing with an addiction for thirty years.

God does not want us to think it cruel to administer physical discipline in a spirit of love and gentleness to our children, as He says in Proverbs 13:24: **"Whoever spares the rod hates his son, but he who loves him is diligent to discipline him."** You may not think that your failure to administer the rod is hateful, but God likens it to hating your child. Strong words indeed, but the understanding is that you should not neglect to physically discipline your child. (In my nearly two decades of counseling addicts, I have learned that neglecting to discipline leads to addictive thinking far more often than parenting that is too strict, though that extreme is damaging, also).

God goes on to encourage parents in Proverbs 22:15: **"Folly is bound up in the heart of a child, but the rod of discipline drives it far from him."** One parental duty is to drive foolishness far from a child. Foolishness is rebellion against God and is clearly visible in Psalm 14:1-2: **"The fool says in his heart, 'There is no God.'**

They are corrupt, they do abominable deeds, there is none who does good. The Lord looks down from heaven on the children of man, to see if there are any who understand, who seek after God." God's rules from His Word are non-negotiable. For example, a child who lies must be disciplined in love for violating one of God's rules (Exodus 20:16). We are to obey His rules because it glorifies Him and is for our own good benefit.

On the other hand, a family's house rules are negotiable, meaning that there are times when these rules can be broken without consequences. That is a parent's prerogative. For example, a house rule may be that a child completes his chores prior to watching television. If a chore is absent-mindedly forgotten rather than a direct disobedient act, then a parent can use wisdom and discretion to not provoke the child to anger. However, if the child is acting disobediently to the house rule in direct, willful defiance to a parent, then the situation now becomes non-negotiable according to Ephesians 6:1: **"Children, obey your parents in the Lord, for this is right."**

When a parents spanks a child who is asking, "Why do you have to spank me, Daddy?" the parent must point the child to the higher authority, Almighty God. The parent can say, "Daddy (or Mommy) must obey God and He commands me to discipline you when you disobey one of His laws. Whenever you disobey God's Word, there are bad consequences that happen as a result of your sinful choice. God wants to spare you these bad consequences."

The child may not understand your explanation entirely. Certainly, he will not like it right away, but you are not trying to be popular with him or spare him the consequences of his actions. Take every opportunity to remind your child that life will offer many choices and that he must consider what will be pleasing to God. Teach him that God is pleased with us when we trust and obey Him because He knows what is best for us. Too many parents want their children to like them and consider them to be "friends." You are the parent and God gave you the authority to discipline your child in love with the rod and reproof.

When a Christian disciplines a child physically with the rod, it is recommended that they do so for <u>disobedient acts</u> and not for <u>accidental childishness</u>. One of our children once rolled and crashed small metal cars against the bedroom wall at age three. We did NOT spank him for tearing up the wall because it was childish playing. He was not being disobedient. He was not doing it in anger or rebellion. We had NOT instructed him in any other way as to how to play properly with his cars, and he thought this was acceptable behavior, so we did not spank. However, we did reprove him by teaching him that he needed to be more aware of how his playing damaged our property. We even launched into a small lesson about stewardship and taking care of what belongs to the Lord. We reproved him because we wanted him to know the seriousness of his childish actions. In the future however, after this instruction had been given, it would have been sinful disobedience for him to repeat playing with his cars in this destructive way, and thus a rod would have been in order. In the case of this child, it never occurred again.

"If left to themselves, children will be rebels, so it is necessary for the parents to train their children. Years ago, the then Duke of Windsor said, 'Everything in the American home is controlled by switches—except the children!'"[16] The Lord does not want you to fear physical correction. Proverbs 23:13 says, **"Do not withhold discipline from a child; if you strike him with a rod, he will not die."** The area of the body perfectly made for physical discipline is the "hiney," as I call it. Your child's "hiney" is commonly called a "bottom," which is the area of the gluteus maximus muscles along with some fat tissue. This part of the body has extra padding that the Creator designed perfectly for protection of the sacrum and spinal cord, but doubles as a perfectly good place to administer physical correction. When a rod is administered to this part of the body three times, the child will not die. We administer three swats of the rod for a disobedient act and only on the "hiney." Do not spank on any other areas of the body. Also, if we ever decide to change the number of swats, we are certain to inform the child exactly how many it will be, so that he or she is prepared to cooperate.

Proverbs 23:14 states: **"If you strike him with the rod, you will save his soul from Sheol."** This proverb tells us that "three swats on the hiney" will ultimately save your child from death and a literal grave (Sheol). In other words, God wants us to have a long-term goal in mind for physical discipline (commonly called a "spanking" though not a biblical term—I prefer "the rod").

---

[16] Wiersbe, W. W. (1996, c1989). *The Bible Exposition Commentary.* 'An exposition of the New Testament comprising the entire 'BE' series'--Jkt. (Eph 6:4). Wheaton, Ill.: Victor Books.

Some parents give a reproof with yelling and screaming that is not gentle in spirit. When a parent yells at a child, it is destructive in many ways. For example, the child is not doing what the parent wants. The parent sees the disobedience of the child, takes the disobedience personally, and then screams at the child. This verbal mistreatment is sinful and counterproductive because it hurts the child's spirit. Proverbs 18:14 states: **"A man's spirit will endure sickness, but a crushed spirit who can bear?"** One of the implications of this verse is that a person's internal, spiritual hurts are more harmful than physical pain stemming from an illness. Spiritual hurts are caused by someone else's sinful choices, such as a parent screaming at a child in out-of-control anger.

Perhaps you know of parents who wrongly think that biting a child that is biting other children is good parenting. Some parents wrongly think that lying to a child so that the child will experience the betrayal of a lie is good parenting. Some parents think rubbing a child's nose in a pool of urine is good parenting when the child wets the bed or misses the toilet. As a parent, you are never to respond to your child's evil choice or troublesome circumstances with evil of your own (Romans 12:21). Never pinch your child after your child pinches someone else! Administer the rod and reproof in a controlled, planned, non-emotional manner as appropriate and God-honoring discipline in love.

The central idea in this chapter is that controlled, purposeful, and gentle-in-spirit physical and verbal discipline is necessary for addiction-proof parenting. The rod is just as vital as the reproof. The child needs reassurance that the rod and reproof are not personal attacks by the parent upon the child; therefore, out-of-control hand beatings are sinful and destructive. God is not pleased with this type of haphazard, raging parenting.

Opponents of administering the rod and reproof fail to see the love in this approach, claiming that it is harmful to a child. That thinking is a product of the new age, postmodern worldly philosophy that permeates our culture today. I challenge you to think biblically about the issue of the rod and reproof and to prayerfully consider implementing it in a manner that pleases the Lord and will help your child to make good choices as an adult.

Conclusion

In conclusion, I want to be honest with you. The rod and reproof chapter was a difficult chapter for me to write. Sometimes, my feelings get in the way of God's truth. I hate to administer the rod to my children. It is the most difficult thing I have ever had to do. I only do it in obedience to God because I trust Him at His Word. I only do it covered with much prayer. I frequently pray by myself before and after I administer the rod and reproof. I always pray with my child after administering the rod. Then I hug and hold the child close to me, often without words.

Do people ever administer the rod hastily or wrongly? Unfortunately, yes. If you do administer it wrongly, repent. Ask the Lord to forgive you and ask your child to forgive you. However, do not allow one wrong experience to determine whether you will administer the rod and reproof in the future. At the end of the day, you must trust God by doing what pleases Him alone. Proverbs 29:17 says it best: **"Discipline your son, and he will give you rest; he will give delight to your heart."** Addiction-proof parenting begins first with obedient parents. Children learn obedience from obedient parents. Children learn to submit to the authority of parents when parents first submit to the authority of God. Modeling good behavior is more powerful than words.

KEY IDEAS AND PRACTICAL THINGS TO DO

1. Read and discuss each proverb presented in this chapter with your child. Allow your child to interact with you and to give examples he has observed of each proverb (i.e. maybe a friend at school disobeyed a teacher demonstrating the folly bound up in the friend's heart).

2. Play the Obedience Game again, but this time, ask your child what should happen if he disobeys the Lord based upon Proverbs 22:15, 23:13-14, and 29:17.

3. Teach your child that God's love does not mean that life will not be unpleasant at times. Read Hebrews 12:3-17 with your child and share how the Lord has disciplined you at times for your disobedience and how it has made you a better person (or more Christ-like). (Do not give details about your sins—be general about sin and specific about God's goodness despite your sin.)

Chapter 6
Physical Touch and Praise

Matt has taken Adderall® since being diagnosed with ADHD in the fifth grade when his parents went through a divorce and Matt struggled to sit still in class. Not knowing what to do, Matt's mom took him to a psychiatrist who prescribed the medication for him. Now, Matt likes to take his own Adderall and buys more of it from other friends who have the same ADHD diagnosis but do not like to take Adderall. Matt has enough to share with Derrick, Raymond, and Freddie who are already drinking alcohol and smoking pot at the party.

Lest you think I am an old-fashioned ogre who only wants to administer the rod of correction and reproof, I want to assure you that is not true. Opposite the rod and reproof are physical touch and praise. For every rod and reproof you administer, you ought to give your child *three times* as much positive, appropriate, physical touch (like a hug) and verbal praise to convey love and reassurance. If all you ever do as a parent is "rod and reprove" your child, you are failing miserably at addiction-proof, biblical parenting. Children crave appropriate physical touch and praise from their parents.

Because children are constantly interpreting life from impressions of people and things around them, they need parents to encourage them when they are walking in the way of wisdom. When your child makes a good choice, praise him for character growth. Let me explain. My wife and I try to refrain from overly-complimenting our girls' outward appearances since the body will pass away (Proverbs 31:30) **"Charm is deceitful, and beauty is vain, but a woman who fears the Lord is to be praised."** Instead, we intentionally strive to compliment their inward character as often as we can according to 1 Peter 3:3-4: **"Do not let your adorning be external—the braiding of hair, the wearing of gold, or the putting on of clothing—but let your adorning be the hidden person of the heart with the imperishable beauty of a gentle and quiet spirit, which in God's sight is very precious."**

In addition, we compliment the children—both girls and boys— when they exhibit the fruit of the Holy Spirit in Galatians 5:22-23: **"love, joy, peace, patience, kindness, goodness, faithfulness, gentleness, and self-control."** We say things like "You were so kind to your sister just now!" or "You were really patient at the doctor's office while Mommy spoke to the doctor today. Thank you!" Furthermore, we use the same words that God uses in His Word so that when they hear a sermon at church, it will make sense. For example, we want our children to know what "covetous" means when they hear it in a sermon at church so we use that word in our home. "Do not covet your brother's toy" is an example of one phrase we say frequently.

Praise the hidden character of your child's heart when the fruit of the Holy Spirit is produced. The best form of praise is when you can give the ultimate glory to God. In addition, if your child learns to play the guitar or piano, praise the Lord for giving the child that wonderful gift. Tell the child that he is talented and gifted by God's grace. The child then learns that the gift comes only from the great gift Giver. Praise your child for inward, spiritual characteristics rather than outward, physical characteristics.

Teach your children the value of *not* praising themselves through bragging. Proverbs 27:2: **"Let another praise you, and not your own mouth; a stranger, and not your own lips."** Boasting is only allowed in the Lord according to 1 Corinthians 1:31: **"Therefore, as it is written, 'Let the one who boasts, boast in the Lord.'"** Encourage your child to acknowledge God in all of his gifts and abilities. Furthermore, the child is to use his gifts to the glory of God and not for selfish gain. For example, do not encourage the guitar-playing child to become a rock star for fame and fortune, but to play the guitar to lead others to worship the Lord.

Verbal praise should be given to the child in order to point them to Christ. He needs to be reminded of God's grace and the gospel as often as you have the opportunity. James 1:17 reminds us that **"every good gift and every perfect gift is from above"** and God is to be praised. Some think that children need verbal praise to pump up their "self-esteem," but that goal is unbiblical. Children need to understand who they are in Christ. Christian children are to die to themselves and to live for Christ. Colossians 3:3 says: **"For you have died, and your life is hidden with Christ in God."** The child's self-worth comes from knowing Christ as Lord and Savior.

Pumping up a child's self-esteem can be destructive. Since all people have selfish, sinful natures, false praise can cause people to make wrong choices. Furthermore, most children are smart enough to know when praise is false. The Bible teaches us to seek out the counsel of others, to be thankful even for the trials in our lives, to submit to the authorities, and not to trust our own understanding. When you teach children that they must feel good about themselves apart from Christ, you are teaching an unbiblical message. You may be teaching them to be prideful and not to humbly trust in God.

The self-esteem movement has been criticized even by *secular* researchers. In an article published in the L.A. Times on January 25, 2005, the writer, Roy F. Baumeister wrote:

> In short, despite the enthusiastic embrace of self-esteem, we found that it conferred only two benefits. It feels good and it supports initiative. Those are nice, but they are far less than we had once hoped for, and it is very questionable whether they justify the effort and expense that schools, parents and therapists have put into raising self-esteem. After all these years, I'm sorry to say, my recommendation is this: Forget about self-esteem and concentrate more on self-control and self-discipline. Recent work suggests this would be good for the individual and good for society—and might even be able to fill some of those promises that self-esteem once made but could not keep.[17]

Baumeister adds that "high self-esteem in schoolchildren does not produce better grades."

So why do we buy into the world's lies? Why do we believe that "self-esteem" is so vital to our children's well-being? It is because we tend to believe the lies we see and hear on television, in books (even "Christian" ones), and the like. Self-esteem is a man-made idea and not a biblical construct. Even many preachers today believe that self-esteem is truth. What a child needs more than self-esteem is "Christ-esteem,"[18] which comes from understanding that we are creatures created for works of righteousness by our Creator, Savior, and Lord. Help your child to understand that he is important to our all-loving God who created him in His own image, though sin has brought the curse of fleshly, selfish living upon us all. God in His grace redeems us from the curse of sin, based upon the sacrifice

[17] Website: http://articles.latimes.com/2005/jan/25/opinion/oe-baumeister25
[18] Term coined by author Dr. Jay Adams who wrote a book with this same name.

of our Lord Jesus upon the cross. For more insight on self-esteem thinking, I recommend the booklet, *Self-Esteem: Are We Really Better Than We Think?* by David Tyler, Focus Publishing.

Conclusion

Teaching your child verbally through appropriate praise that points him to God should be coupled with appropriate physical touch. Kissing your child on the cheek, hugging him, and holding him in your arms are all important ways to reassure him of your love and even God's love Resting your hand on his shoulder during a group conversation is a subtle but strong affirmation of your love for him. Again, I recommend that you physically touch your child at least *three times* as often as you administer the rod and reproof. Celebrate with your children the obedient successes in life by physically touching them appropriately. There are many ways to appropriately love your child with physical touch (like a "high five"). Take the opportunities that come your way to biblically praise and physically touch your child as frequently as you can. He will not be young for long.

KEY IDEAS AND PRACTICAL THINGS TO DO

1. Make a list of your child's strengths, abilities, and gifts. Ask Him to do the same about himself. (Note: if your child is not old enough, then make the list with your child). Pray and thank the Lord for each one of those strengths, abilities, and gifts.

2. Purpose to display appropriate affection in hugs, holding, sitting close to, putting your hand on a shoulder, etc. at least once per day (if not many more times!).

3. Read Proverbs 17:22 with your child: **"A joyful heart is good medicine, but a crushed spirit dries up the bones."** Make a list of things you can do together to bring more laughter into your relationship.

Chapter 7
A Balanced Approach

At the party, Matt and Freddie leave Derrick and Raymond who offer a marijuana cigarette to the four girls Raymond brought to the party. Three of the girls smoke a joint together but Edna, the fourth girl, says "No, thanks." Edna remembered that her parents literally said that they would "kill her" if they ever caught her drinking or drugging.

By God's perfect design, two parents are to raise a child and provide a balanced approach to discipline and biblical parenting. Often one parent is more gracious and lenient while the other is more strict and rigid. Parents must work together and strive to be balanced. After a disciplinary event occurs, parents must communicate privately (without the children present) and discuss the pros and cons of the situation. They must be humble and willing to learn from the other parent who may have a very different viewpoint. Parenting is teamwork at its best and sometimes at its worst. Nothing binds a husband and wife closer together in their marriage than the prayerful desire to influence their children for God. Children are naturally good at dividing parents who are not diligently maintaining unified goals and direction. A lack of unity in parenting can contribute to making a bad marriage worse.

Single parents have my utmost respect. I realize daily how much I need my wife to balance my parenting approach, and she would say the same thing. Many single parents depend daily upon the grace of God and often do a better job of parenting than two parents who refuse to work together in unity and therefore undermine one another. However, in our fallen world, many children are in single parent homes and some of them are missing a key ingredient in the parenting process. When two parents work together, there is strength in numbers and a child receives the best balance of both worlds. Parents who may err on each extreme (grace or justice) but who communicate well and work at maintaining unity offer their children a balanced approach of the truth presented in love that models Jesus Christ.

When He walked the earth as fully man and fully God, Jesus Christ was perfectly balanced. Jesus was 100% man and 100% divine at the same time. Only God can fully understand how this occurred because it is a supra-logical concept, or beyond mankind's ability to reason. Furthermore, Jesus was balanced in another way. He was 100% gracious and 100% truthful with everyone He encountered and in every situation. John 1:14 confirms His perfect balance: **"And the Word became flesh and dwelt among us, and we have seen his glory, glory as of the only Son from the Father, full of grace and truth."**

Like Jesus, you are to be balanced when you deal with others, especially your children. You must strive to be both truthful and gracious because doing so best reflects the balanced nature of God who was also perfectly just and merciful at the same time. Your goal as a human parent is to point your child to his Heavenly Parent, God. Ephesians 4:15 states it this way: **"Rather, speaking the truth in love, we are to grow up in every way into him who is the head, into Christ."** Strive to be balanced by speaking the truth in love to your child at all times so that your child will grow spiritually.

Positive and Negative Instruction

Teach your child the "put-off" and "put-on" concept that pleases the Lord. Ephesians 4:22-24 states: **"to put off your old self, which belongs to your former manner of life and is corrupt through deceitful desires, and to be renewed in the spirit of your minds, and to put on the new self, created after the likeness of God in true righteousness and holiness."** When we become Christians, the Bible tells us to put off our old thoughts, words, and actions; to be renewed in our thinking about that old desire; and to put on new thoughts, words, and actions that are pure, righteous, and holy. For example, we are to put off our old behaviors of stealing and replace them with new behaviors of working hard and giving to others. Ephesians 4:28 is the source of this example: **"Let the thief no longer steal, but rather let him labor, doing honest work with his own hands, so that he may have something to share with anyone in need."**

Replacing bad habits is a key element in biblical, addiction-proof parenting. Habits are never broken. Instead, they are replaced. Bad habits, like stealing, are to be replaced by work and giving (Ephesians 4:28). Bad habits, like thoughts of envy, are to be replaced with godly thoughts of gratitude for everything God has given us, and ultimately for our Savior. Bad habits, like saying "You are stupid," are to be replaced with godly words like, "You are kind." This put-off and put-on principle is powerful and highly effective in parenting.

However, there is one additional part to the put-off and put-on principle, and that is to be renewed in the spirit of our minds (Ephesians 4:23). Mind renewal is essential for all change. Mind renewal can be summed up simply in this way: you now hate what you once loved (sinful put-off) and you now love what you once hated (righteous put-on). For a drug addict, mind renewal toward one's drug of choice is to hate that particular drug because of its damaging consequences and to embrace a drug-free life devoted to Christ because of its benefits and purpose of glorifying the Lord. When you parent, you must help your child to embrace godliness (i.e. loving the new "put-on") and to reject selfish, sinful desires (i.e. hating the "put-off").

Because all children are born with a sinful nature, they must be renewed in the spirit of their minds, which only comes from the Holy Spirit's power in accordance with the principles of God's Word. You must first learn God's Word for yourself to be able to properly teach it to your child. The books of Proverbs and James are excellent places to start when teaching your child what is right and what is wrong. You do not have to be a biblical scholar; you only need to be one step ahead of your child. Therefore, study a Bible lesson in advance of teaching it to your child and teach what you learned from it.

Remember that the goal is to be balanced in your parenting by teaching the child what must be done (instruction/admonition) and what must not be done (discipline), in accordance to Ephesians 6:4: **"Fathers, do not provoke your children to anger, but bring them up in the discipline and instruction of the Lord."** A parent failing to do either part of this verse (the discipline or the instruction of the child in the Lord) will "provoke" the child "to anger" (Ephesians 6:4). The phrase "bring them up" in this verse means to nourish the child spiritually. Nourishment is spiritual food from the Word of God that provides sustenance for the child. Without nurturing him in both discipline and instruction, he will be spiritually malnourished. As he grows physically older into adulthood, a malnourished child will turn to temporal, physical objects for spiritual fulfillment. These objects often include drugs and other types of "addictive" pleasures.

I've discovered this to be true with the hundreds of addicts I've counseled. Many of them were left to themselves, never disciplined, never instructed or admonished. Instead they were "spoiled rotten" and rescued from negative consequences during their teen years. They were given material things without the responsibility that goes with them, and never given the rod or reproof. They were spiritually malnourished and spiritually neglected. They were left alone to believe that the world existed for them and their desires for pleasure. They developed a "worship disorder" in that they sought spiritual fulfillment and nourishment from physical, idolatrous pleasures that led to emptiness, despair, entrapment, physical addiction, deception, and anger. *Physical things never fulfill one's spiritual appetite to worship and serve the Lord.*

A child must learn that he is not the center of the universe. This starts in the home. Parents must teach children that they are part of a bigger thing called the family, the church, and society. These organized bodies exist for the child but only function properly when each person involved in that body thinks of others more than thinking of self. According to Philippians 2:3-4, your child is to: **"Do nothing from rivalry or conceit, but in humility count others more significant than yourselves. Let each of you look not only to his own interests, but also to the interests of others."** Are you teaching your child to serve others? Do you have a child-centered home or a Christ-centered home?

Parents have the primary responsibility for teaching children to serve others. The Church is helpful in reinforcing this teaching but the Lord places the responsibility for the spiritual development of children upon the parents. In these two verses of Philippians 2, the word "rivalry" is used and has to do with competition. In the United States, our culture is very competitive and often individualistic. Be careful that you are not instilling a "win at all costs" attitude of rivalry in your child that will carry over into other areas in life and keep him from being a "team player." Children must learn to value others, especially those who have different gifts than they have, and a wrong emphasis upon competition and winning will diminish that lesson (Philippians 2:3-4).

We are called to function as the body of Christ. Sometimes competitive sport mindsets detract from the idea of being part of a bigger body. In 1 Corinthians 12:18-27, the Bible states:

> **But as it is, God arranged the members in the body, each one of them, as he chose. If all were a single member, where would the body be? As it is, there are many parts, yet one body. The eye cannot say to**

> the hand, "I have no need of you," nor again the head to the feet, "I have no need of you." On the contrary, the parts of the body that seem to be weaker are indispensable, and on those parts of the body that we think less honorable we bestow the greater honor, and our unpresentable parts are treated with greater modesty, which our more presentable parts do not require. But God has so composed the body, giving greater honor to the part that lacked it, that there may be no division in the body, but that the members may have the same care for one another. If one member suffers, all suffer together; if one member is honored, all rejoice together. Now you are the body of Christ and individually members of it.

Teach your child to put forth his best effort at all times for the glory of God as his primary motivation (1 Corinthians 10:31) and not for the motivation of "winning at all costs." Because of the preponderance of sport teams in the U.S.A., this part of addiction-proof parenting needs to be addressed. Teach your child to play hard but to leave the results up to God. Also, teach him to be a good winner and a good loser, being gracious to others despite the outcome. Humility and grace are attitudes God wants His children to have. Sport teams can be a blessing or a curse depending on how parents and coaches emphasize the importance of spiritual outcomes (i.e. humility, gratitude, submission, effort, and good sportsmanship) over physical outcomes (i.e. winning the game and scoring the most points). Remember that James 4:6b states: **"God opposes the proud, but gives grace to the humble."**

Being Like Christ is the Goal

The Gospel message is balanced. The Gospel tells us that we are all sinners (Romans 3:23) in need of God's saving grace found only by faith in Christ Jesus, who paid for our sins with His own life. Quite simply, your child is a sinner in need of a Savior, and God has provided that Savior by grace through faith in Jesus Christ (Ephesians 2:8-9). Point your child to a relationship with Christ where he will find true intimacy, fulfillment, self-worth, and value. In a world full of fanciful superheroes like Batman, Superman, Wonder Woman, and the like, your child's number one hero must be Jesus Christ! Your child should emulate Jesus and have a strong desire to be like Him! Christ is the only Person worthy of being our hero, as He teaches us a new way to be human: full of grace and full of truth (John 1:14). The book of Hebrews holds up examples of human heroes—not perfect—but growing in faith. These make good lessons and food for thought.

When teaching your children about being like Christ, remind them that Jesus never sinned or hurt anyone. Jesus can be emulated because He always did and said what was right in a loving way. Your child can read the Gospels and see God manifest before his eyes. Teach him to value the things of God and he will value Christ more. Remind him that overcoming evil with good (Romans 12:21) is real super-heroism!

When you deal with your child's sin, do not leave him there to wallow in sin and self-pity. Many "addicts" are mired in self-pity. Instead, tell them about the forgiveness only found in Jesus Christ. Teach him about the grace and mercy of God. James 4:6b states: **"God opposes the proud, but gives grace to the humble."** Address the sin issue, but if you neglect to spiritually feed your child the biblical principles of the forgiveness and grace of God, then you will leave him without hope. He will remain in sin. Instead, pray with your child. Lead him in a prayer asking forgiveness of God through Christ for that sin. *Help him to learn more about the grace of God by experiencing the grace of God through you.* Did you catch that? Allow Christ to be gracious through you which means you must be gracious and merciful with your child! Then, do not bring up that matter again since it has been forgiven. Referring back to Ephesians 6:4, Warren Wiersbe states in his commentary:

> Fathers provoke their children and discourage them by saying one thing and doing another—by always blaming and never praising, by being inconsistent and unfair in discipline, and by showing favoritism in the home, by making promises and not keeping them, and by making light of problems that, to the children, are very important. Christian parents need the fullness of the Spirit so they can be sensitive to the needs and problems of their children.[19]

---

[19] Wiersbe, W. W. (1996, c1989). *The Bible Exposition Commentary.* "An exposition of the New Testament comprising the entire 'BE' series"--Jkt. (Ephesians 6:4). Wheaton, Ill.: Victor Books.

How gracious are you with your children? Do they see God's grace from your words and actions toward them? Are the fruits of the Spirit evident in your life so that your children may see Christ in you (Galatians 5:22-23)? Remember that your job as a parent is to point them to their Heavenly Father as the only perfect Parent who perfectly loves them. You must be what you want your children to be.

Many reading this book may be thinking that addiction-proof, biblical parenting is too hard and not realistic. Let me assure you that you can do all of this if you submit to God and allow Him to do it through you and by the might of His Spirit. God will provide the grace you need as a parent when you faithfully, diligently, patiently, and obediently practice this type of balanced discipline. Rarely does anyone play Mozart the first time they sit down at the piano. It takes practice and sometimes years of practice to become the parent God wants you to be, but it starts now in the "small" and seemingly unimportant moments of your life. Strive to be the best parent you can be moment by moment and watch what the Lord will do in your life.

Developing Christ-likeness

As a parent, you must be like Jesus' parents who were obedient to God's laws as evidenced in Luke 2:22-24, 2:27, 2:39, and 2:42. Jesus' parents obeyed the Word of God and it impacted Jesus greatly in His development as a man. Take your children to church worship services and church events but remember that home is the most important environment to daily teach them about the Gospel and the grace of God. Conflicts with siblings and friends provide excellent opportunities for teachable moments. Connect your children's spirituality with the everyday moments of their lives.

As fully man and fully God, Jesus was an example of the most balanced growth and development of any child ever. In Luke 2:52, it states: **"And Jesus increased in wisdom and in stature and in favor with God and man."** Jesus grew in wisdom (intellectually), in stature (physically), in favor with God (spiritually), and in favor with man (socially). It is a parent's responsibility to provide the best environment possible for a child to develop in these same areas:

Parents are responsible for the intellectual development of their child. Be sure you provide your child with adequate resources for intellectual development. Personally, I prefer homeschooling or a private Christian school, but not all parents are able to take those options. Just be warned that if you send your child to a public school, you must be more diligent to undo some of the false teachings that will impact your child's faith in God, such as evolution, abortion, and the like. As one who attended public schools for my entire education, I know I was indoctrinated and believed many worldly ideas that contradict Christianity. Thankfully, my parents helped me to put off many of those worldly ideas and to put on biblical truths to replace them. My wife continues to help me when those worldly mindsets creep back into my thinking!

Parents are responsible for the physical development of their child. This includes a nutritious diet, proper sleep and rest, and appropriate exercise as recommended by your pediatrician. Just like adults, a child's appetite is developed by acquiring a taste for certain foods. For example, a child who is primarily fed fruits and vegetables when young will develop a taste for those foods. If a child is fed chocolate and sweets when young, they will develop a taste for those foods. Parents cultivate the appetite and desire for food by what they feed their child when they are young. To illustrate, one of my children refuses to eat chocolate. When young, this child was not given anything sweet to eat for two years except for a cake at the one year old birthday party. Nearly a decade later, this child refuses most sweets and especially chocolate![20] (Chocolate is not sinful in itself. It is another area that needs to be approached in moderation; an opportunity to train a child to make moderation in food choices a goal).

Parents are responsible for the spiritual growth of their child. Children are like sponges for spiritual things. They want answers to their questions. In fact, I think children are often more receptive to biblical teachings and spiritual truths than adults. In other words, the spiritual ground is more fertile in children! Unfortunately, some parents "un-god" the normal thoughts of God in their children by a lack of obedience to the Scriptures and a failure to teach their children biblical truths. Do not allow wrong thoughts about God to go by unchecked. Cultivate thoughts of God based upon Scripture beginning in Genesis. Remind your child of the blessings of God who is his Creator, Sustainer, and Redeemer. Promote thankfulness

---

[20] Lest you think I am boasting, we did not do this same thing with some of the others and they love chocolate. We are far from perfect parents, I assure you!

in his heart. Remember, everyday events are an opportunity to point your child to eternity with God.

Parents are responsible for promoting the proper social development of their child. Teach your child proper manners, how to make eye contact, how to interact appropriately with strangers, to respect adults, and how to be kind to others. Teach them to pray for those who do not know Christ and are spiritually lost. Most children develop socially on their own and often in a negative manner. Teach your child how to be a good friend to others and he will have friends. Remind him of the dangers of peer pressure and the importance of doing what pleases God first. Galatians 1:10 states: **"For am I now seeking the approval of man, or of God? Or am I trying to please man? If I were still trying to please man, I would not be a servant of Christ."**

Peer pressure is a constant concern. Parents must help their children to choose their friends. Sometimes, a parent must intervene and insist that the child not spend time with another child who is a bad influence. I understand that children make poor choices occasionally; however, what I am referring to is a child who is disobedient, rebellious, and a scoffer. Parents have the God-given authority to step in and to protect their children from such influences. To fail to do so is sinful. 1 Corinthians 15:33 reminds parents: **"Do not be deceived: 'Bad company ruins good morals.'"** This verse warns us not to deceive ourselves into thinking that our children are going to be a good influence upon rebels and scoffers. Instead, the Bible tells us that bad companions and friendships will ruin your child's good morals. I have had many parents confess to me that they allowed their teens to hang around with the wrong crowd and that it led to using drugs and alcohol.

Take the authority God has given you as a parent and provide safety, wisdom, and opportunities for growth for your child. Limit the amount of television you allow your children to watch. Limit the time you allow them to play video games. Discipline your children by having them sit still and read a book (or look at pictures for non-readers) for fifteen to thirty minutes at a time. Reward them when they obediently sit quietly for that amount of time reading a book. Many of those who have problems with addiction despise reading. Many say their parents never made them read. When this is the case with one of my counselees, it is very difficult for them to overcome their flesh and begin reading the Bible. Scripture reading is the

Christian's number one weapon for tearing down the lies of Satan and this world in order to overcome an addiction of any type.

Conclusion

A balanced approach to parenting full of grace and truth provides a child with the best opportunity to succeed in a fallen world filled with the traps of Satan that appeal to the flesh. Discipline your child in a balanced way that best exemplifies Jesus Christ for the glory of God and for the benefit of your beloved offspring. Your child's hero must be Jesus Christ, the "coolest" person that ever walked the planet! Jesus teaches us a new way to be human: Spirit-filled, embracing the truth, surrendered to God, and loving toward others.

KEY IDEAS AND PRACTICAL THINGS TO DO

1. Assess whether you are better at being gracious or truthful. Nearly everyone falls to one of these two sides: grace or truth. List several ways you can work on becoming more balanced at expressing both of these to become more like Christ (John 1:14).

2. Think about how you and your child fit into the body of Christ. What are your spiritual gifts? What do you offer your church? Do something together as a family or as a parent-child team to bless your pastor, a member of your church, or the church body in general.

3. Evaluate your child's growth in the areas of Luke 2:52: intellectual (wisdom), physical (stature), spiritual (favor with God), and social (favor with man). You can use a scale from 1 to 10 (10 being excellent, 1 being very poor). Ask your child to rate himself, too. Develop a practical plan for growing in all four of these areas (i.e. read a book, including the Bible, exercise, pray, and spend time with a friend at your home).

Section 2

The Biblical Approach to "Addiction"

Chapter 8
Understanding "Addiction"

Edna wants to go home from the party but she sees that her ride, Raymond, has already become too intoxicated to drive home. Edna's friends encourage her to "just try it with us one time" referring to the marijuana. "Its fun," one friend said, "and it will make you giggle a lot." Edna looks at her friends and considers it for a minute. "My parents are always asleep when I get home anyway," she thinks to herself.

From this point forward, we will focus on the biblical approach to addiction and how to recognize and prevent your child from developing the mindset of an "addict." The tone of the book will be more serious simply because I see the wreckage of idolatry and "addiction" nearly each day as I am privileged to conduct biblical counseling. At times, I wish I could go back in time, and teach the parents of those people some biblical parenting strategies, to avoid having to deal with the terrible impact of addictive choices. For this reason, I hope you are ready to implement some new approaches in your God-given call to parenting.

If it were up to me, I would always put quotation marks around the word "addiction." Let me explain. "Addiction" is a worldly term and as such it is defined as the "persistent *compulsive* use of a substance known by the user to be harmful."[21] The key word is "compulsive," which implies that one is not responsible for his addictive choices because he cannot help himself. This is not true, because in the early stages of addiction wrong choices are often made with a planned purpose to escape from the problems and sorrows of life. A "compulsive" behavior is defined as "an irresistible impulse to perform an irrational act."[22] But ask yourself: is the choice to fulfill the desire of an addiction in fact *irresistible*? Usually the choice is planned. It may *seem* unconscious and unplanned but there is much thinking involved. The addict does make irrational choices to sin in that the addictive choices often (1) do not make sense, (2) give temporary pleasure only, and (3) result in heartache once the pleasure disappears. Using my definition of addiction I would say

---

[21] Merriam-Webster, Inc. *Merriam-Webster's Collegiate Dictionary.* Includes Index. 10th ed. Springfield, Mass., U.S.A.: Merriam-Webster, 1996, c1993.
[22] Ibid.

these choices become habitual, but they are not compulsive.

In this section, my desire is for the Lord to open your eyes to gain insights into the heart of addiction—into the heart attitudes, thinking, and emotions of anyone who is enslaved to an addiction. How does an addict think? Parents must understand how certain things they do may be fostering an addictive mindset in their children. Children and teens who become addicted think in five basic worldly and self-centered mindsets that I have termed:

1. Entitlement
2. Consumer
3. Victim
4. Perishing
5. Rebellious

The first two mentalities are based upon Matthew 22:37-40 and the last three are based upon Ephesians 5:18-21. Each of these has a positive corresponding biblical alternative of:

1. Be Humble
2. Be Giving
3. Be Responsible
4. Be Grateful
5. Be Submissive

These five new antidotal mindsets can be instilled in children at very young ages by committed parents in order to train their children to avoid addictive thinking.

Basic Biblical Concepts Related to Addiction

You must first understand the basics about "addiction" from a biblical perspective in order to best provide addiction-proof parenting for your child. Worldly ideas about addiction are dominant in today's culture and even in Christian churches. Often, these worldly ideas about addiction are in direct conflict with the Holy Scriptures yet the church still embraces some of them! Therefore, I urge you to begin thinking about them from a biblical perspective rather than from a worldly perspective. You will have more success as a parent when you stick to God's Word rather than man's best ideas.

In *The Heart of Addiction*, addiction is defined as the "persistent *habitual* use of a substance known by the user to be harmful."[23] Addictive thinking and behaviors do not make sense to those who love and observe an addict. Why would someone do something they know will end up harming them? Unfortunately, pain and suffering often do not deter an "addict" from pursuing a drug of choice.

The addicted mind is consumed with one thing: pleasing self. There is a pursuit of avoiding pain and seeking pleasure at any cost, which usually includes losing close relationships with loved ones. The desire for immediate gratification seems overwhelming to them, especially when painful withdrawal symptoms are occurring. In drug addiction those withdrawal symptoms include vomiting, headaches, deep depression, and flu-like symptoms that are often severe. Physical dependence upon a drug develops over time and is called "tolerance." Different drugs affect people differently in terms of tolerance and withdrawal symptoms. With "addictions" related to gambling, spending money, self-injury, etc., the withdrawal is more emotional than physical.

The physical problems associated with addiction lead many people to believe that it is merely a medical illness. Some even suggest it is a "genetic, brain disease" though no scientific proof has been provided to substantiate these claims. Ever since the 1930's, most of the world has believed the medical model theorists who say that addiction is a "disease," that it is progressive and not curable. Where is the hope in the mindset of a progressive, incurable disease?

Many people do not think of addiction as a moral problem since the world says that an addict is not responsible for acquiring the supposed "disease." However, though the person supposedly did not do anything to acquire the disease of addiction, (alcoholism, for example) they are responsible to "treat the disease" by going to self-help meetings and staying clean and sober. Self-help meetings are the so-called "medicine" necessary to treat "addiction" problems in the world's approach.

My question of this approach is: if it is not my responsibility for becoming "addicted," then why do I have to take responsibility for

---

[23] Shaw, Mark. *The Heart of Addiction*, Focus Publishing, Bemidji, MN, p. 28. For a deeper study of "addiction," I recommend you read my other books on that subject as well, since I can only give you a general overview in this one chapter.

treating my "addiction" now? That very idea causes a bitter spirit in many addicts who think that this world created by God has given them a raw deal—actually suggesting that they are being wronged! It is a lie. In fact, the opposite is true. If anything, God is being gracious to those who really are responsible for the sinful choices that led to a physical and mental addiction. A person is prone to sin—that is, missing God's desired standard of righteousness—and that sin is enjoyable and becomes "addictive" in that sense.

The question is not: "Why is God torturing me and allowing me to have this disease of addiction?"

The question is: "Why does a just and righteous God not strike me dead for my sinful attitude and wrong choices to sin?" Can you see the opposite attitudes behind these two questions? Do you see how the view of God is radically different in each of these questions?

The world's way of dealing with the problem is often confusing because it comes across as "double speak." The world says to the addict, "You have a disease and there is no hope, but you can treat it with self-help meetings every week for the rest of your life." There is only a reference to a "higher power" in the world's solution, and not necessarily the Creator who is Jesus Christ. Furthermore, the world's approach to addiction is not scientific fact, though it is often accepted and presented as such. It is merely man's theory about the problem and it is even criticized by secularists who see through its hypocrisy.[24]

The world accepts the idea of addiction as a disease simply because people do not want to blame themselves for the problem and they deny Christ as the solution. "I only tried my drug of choice once and then I was hooked" is a comment you might hear from someone who has bought into the idea of addiction as a disease. "It's not my fault (or choice) that I'm addicted." While there is a physical component to drug addiction, the implication is that one's DNA, brain, environment, family of origin, upbringing, and other factors *cause* one to be addicted. Therefore, the disease concept makes sense when it is taught at self-help meetings and in secular treatment

---

[24] A book written by a secular psychiatrist, Dr. Lance Dodes, does a solid job of critiquing "addiction" as a disease. Ironically, the name of his book is the same name of my book, *The Heart of Addiction*. While I disagree with Dr. Dodes' secular perspective, I did find some common ground with his constructive criticisms.

programs. It fosters a "victim mentality" in people who are being programmed to think about it in this way. The biblical approach is rarely presented, and when it is, it is misrepresented and twisted to seem archaic and mean-spirited.

Ironically, many who are involved in self-help meetings see the solution to addiction as a *spiritual awakening*; however, the world's ideas of a spiritual awakening are devoid of God as our loving Creator and are different from a Christian's ideas of spiritual awakening. The two approaches are fundamentally opposed, yet they both recognize the solution to the problem as being "spiritual" in nature.

A Spiritual Battle

The biblical approach to addiction is absolutely spiritual, since it is the Holy Spirit who must perform spiritual "heart surgery" to transform an addict from selfish living to selfless living. A life lived to fulfill what the Bible calls "the flesh" (now called "addiction" according to the world's terminology) must be replaced with a desire to "walk in the Spirit."[25] The biblical approach to addiction is defined in the Holy Scriptures. Though physical problems manifest, an addiction is simply a "physical symptom of a deeper, spiritual problem of the attitudes of the heart generally called 'idolatry' in the Bible."[26] It is a <u>sinful nature</u> problem—not a disease problem. We are born in sin with a selfish disposition toward pleasing ourselves. Addiction is simply a manifestation of our sinful hearts. Therefore, the heart of "addiction" is sin and it is a "worship disorder."

Let us pause for a moment and further explore what we mean by "worship disorder." Your child has been created by God to worship Him alone, yet he is worshiping the wrong person—himself! What happens when a child is caught up in any addiction and idolatrous desire is that he becomes consumed with self so that other people become simply objects to them. By objects, I mean that addicts desire for other people to serve them and their idolatrous desires. Idolatry is a difficult concept for some to understand today. Simply put, idolatry is the worship of a false god. This false god can be anything that takes a higher place in our thoughts and lives than the Lord God Jehovah.

---

[25] Read Romans 8 for more about "the flesh" and the "indwelling" of the Holy Spirit.

[25] Shaw, Mark. *The Heart of Addiction*, Focus Publishing, Bemidji, MN, pp. viii-ix.

False gods in our culture today are not little wooden statues but are simply the love of money, pleasure, and power, the love of the esteem of others, love of gambling, shopping, video games, sexual immorality, and the love of drugs and alcohol, to name only a few. Idols come in many shapes and sizes but they all have one thing in common: they are desired because of how they please *me*! In other words, the heart of idolatry is always selfish motive for selfish gain.

Therefore, others must also bow down and worship the idolater's idol.[27] For example, in terms of addiction, family members of the addict are expected to help them with finances, transportation, and to support their desire to fulfill the idolatrous pursuit. If a family member helps them to satisfy the idolatrous desire, then that person is viewed as an "enabler" and will be allowed to remain in their life. However, if they refuse to help the addict satisfy their desires then that person is viewed as an "obstacle" and will not be included often in their daily life.[28]

You can observe these behaviors in children when they don't get what they want. Unless this sinful idolatry is recognized and addressed by parents, these behaviors will continue on into adulthood in more determined yet subtle ways.

It is really sad to watch someone pursue an activity or drug of choice so much that they are willing to allow close relationships to be destroyed. But pain and suffering often do not deter an addict from seeking fleeting pleasures. In this way, addiction is simply a form of the ancient concept of idolatry. It remains a worship disorder in the heart of the sinful addict who is not living to please God but to please self.

As a parent, I urge you to call these actions what God calls them: sin. There is a solution to every sin! The forgiveness of the Lord Jesus Christ is available to sinners saved by the grace of God through faith in Christ (Ephesians 2:8-9). Calling the behavior "sin" is not mean-spirited but is truthful and liberating once a person understands the gospel message and the faithfulness of God to forgive our sins. 1 John 1:9 states: **"If we confess our sins, he is faithful and just to forgive us our sins and to cleanse us from all unrighteousness."**

---

[27] Sande, Ken. *The Peacemaker*. Baker Books, Grand Rapids, MI, pp. 102-109.

[28] More on this subject can be read in my book, *Divine Intervention*, in chapter 1 particularly.

As mentioned earlier, "addiction" is simply a violation of the first of the Ten Commandments: **"You shall have no other gods before Me"** (Exodus 20:3). When a drug or activity is pursued to the sacrifice of relationships and responsibilities, this first commandment is broken. The drug has become this person's source of all comfort and pleasure and serves as a "false god." This is the definition of idolatry. When spending money is out of control to the sacrifice of relationships and responsibilities, it is a violation of the first commandment. When gambling, self-injuring, videogame playing, sexually immoral behavior, and overeating are excessively pursued to the sacrifice of relationships and responsibilities, the thinking and behaviors associated with these pleasures are a violation of the first commandment which is simply "idolatry."

The truth is that any pleasure that is excessively pursued to satisfy our thoughts and behaviors is idolatry. One of my favorite preachers said that we are all "idol factories," meaning that we are capable of producing new idols in our hearts in mass quantities.[29] I think you can see why the biblical counseling ministry of Truth In Love Ministries[30] will never lack for counselees while idolatry and all types of "addictions" are so prevalent. The world is continually categorizing all of these types of "addictions" into separate behavioral categories when the heart issue is really the same. The consequences of various "addictions" may be quite diverse; however, the sinful, idolatrous heart of mankind is always the same.

When you think biblically, there is no need to categorize each type of addiction because they are all violations of the first commandment to have no other gods before the Lord.[31] In the New Testament, Jesus restated this commandment in the affirmative in Matthew 22:37-40: **"And he said to him, 'You shall love the Lord your God with all your heart and with all your soul and with all your mind. This is the great and first commandment. And a second is like it: You shall love your neighbor as yourself. On these two commandments**

---

[29] Taken from several teachings and sermons from Pastor/Teacher Harry Reeder at Briarwood Presbyterian Church.

[30] www.histruthinlove.org

[31] Sadly, many self-help groups that have developed to address each specific area of "addiction"—gambling, overeating, alcohol, cocaine, narcotics, and others treat the outward behavior and not the heart of the problem. What's worse is that some who attend alcohol self-help groups do NOT want those who attend cocaine self-help groups to attend their meetings.

depend all the Law and the Prophets.'" Jesus told us to love God as our first priority and love others as much as we love ourselves.

Not only are we to refrain from having other gods before Him, we are to love Him with all our heart. Therefore, we must run from any idolatrous desire that seeks to displace God from His rightful place in our hearts. We must also love others as much as we already love ourselves, which means to serve them by putting their needs as equal to our own. In fact, believers are called to count others as more important than themselves: **"Do nothing from rivalry or conceit, but in humility count others more significant than yourselves."**[32]

When someone is caught up in an active addiction, they are most certainly failing to love God and others more than loving self. The actively "addicted" person is seeking the drug or activity of choice more than they are seeking God and they are willing to be selfish in order to get what they desire. They will steal, kill, destroy their relationships with others and act just like Satan. Jesus said in John 10:10: **"The thief comes only to steal and kill and destroy. I came that they may have life and have it abundantly."** "Addiction" is satanic by this very definition and leads to utter destruction (Ephesians 5:18), whereas a life lived by abiding in Christ leads to abundant life now and eternally.

A life lived selfishly is one lived as if there is no God. Scripture calls this person a "fool" in Psalm 14:1a: **"The fool says in his heart, 'There is no God.' They are corrupt, they do abominable deeds, there is none who does good."** A fool is not stupid or unintelligent; rather, a fool is a rebel who denies the truth that there is a higher being to whom he will give an account in eternity. As Christians we know that the "higher being" is Jesus Christ and it is our relationship with Him that will determine our eternal destiny.

Conclusion

Many mistakenly think the "heart" is only the emotions of a person. However, the mind and the heart are connected in the inner person so that when you read "mind," think "heart," and vice-versa. The word "heart" in the Bible is not referring to the blood pumping, beating organ in your chest but the "soul or mind, as it is the fountain and seat of the thoughts, passions, desires, appetites, affections,

---

[32] Philippians 2:3

purposes, and endeavors."[33] Sinners in need of God's saving grace must have spiritual heart surgery performed by the Great Physician, God Himself. Thankfully, the Lord Jesus Christ is still in the business of radical heart change for anyone, including addicts. Teach your child the difference between "recovery" and transformation. Teach them the biblical approach to addiction—total transformation—not the world's approach which is to battle and to cope with a problem but never overcome it.

KEY IDEAS AND PRACTICAL THINGS TO DO

1. While under the care of a physician, take your medications properly. Teach your child that medications are a blessing from God but that we are ultimately depending upon the Lord to help us through His divinely appointed means. Be informative when you communicate about medications to be certain your children understand the proper use of them.

2. Play cooperation games with your child to promote teamwork rather than competition. While there is a place for competition, many children compare themselves to others and are overly competitive, which hinders their ability to be good teammates. The Lord wants us to see ourselves as part of the body of Christ and not competitive against that body like a group of cancerous cells. (For example, we play "team" solitaire where we put the aces in the middle and try to work together to beat "Sol" by playing all of our cards. Modify games that are competitive into cooperation games.)

---

[33] Strong, J. 1996. The Exhaustive Concordance of the Bible: Showing every word of the text of the common English version of the canonical books, and every occurrence of each word in regular order (electronic ed.). Woodside Bible Fellowship: Ontario.

3. Make a list of things you once idolized. For example, your list might include a car you wanted, a game you had to buy, a music CD, a DVD, etc. Next to each item, after you received it, did you cherish each item more or less—write yes or no. Share these stories with your child, talking about the temporary satisfaction of things and the lasting satisfaction of knowing God.

Chapter 9
What a Transformation Looks Like

Walking past Edna, two of the boys, Freddie and Matt, are joking and pushing each other. They are holding water balloons and preparing to throw them into a big group of people who are standing around the keg. Launching the balloons, the circle scatters with several people getting soaked. Freddie and Matt laugh hysterically until two guys from that broken circle come running after them and tackle them. Freddie and Matt find themselves on the ground in a wrestling match with the two guys at the side of the house.

"Recovery" is the buzz word in secular addiction counseling. "Recovery" means to "regain" or to recapture one's old self.[34] In the physical realm it is a good word to describe a medical condition. The nature of the word implies that our "old self" was healthy and good. In the spiritual world, God knows that is not the case, and He desires more for us. Even the word "reform" is inadequate for what God desires to do in an addict's heart because to "reform" something is simply "to change into an improved form or condition."[35] To "transform" something is to "change" its "character or condition."[36]

God has given us a great example of transformation in nature. The lowly caterpillar is an amazing example of transformation and one that will teach your child the practical lesson of trusting God. For one thing, only God can bring about this transformation.

You can tie little wings on a caterpillar and drop him out of an upstairs window, but he will only fall flat on the ground. You may "recover" the little guy, dust him off and restore him to his old self, but you have not changed his character. The truth is that even he cannot change his character by himself. But one day, an inner change begins to take place and out of some miraculous happening, he is radically transformed into a new creature that is a beautiful moth or butterfly.

---

[34] Merriam-Webster, I. 1996, c1993. *Merriam-Webster's Collegiate Dictionary.* Includes Index. (10th ed.). Merriam-Webster: Springfield, Mass., U.S.A.
[35] Ibid.
[36] Ibid.

In a similar way, God demonstrates a transformation even more amazing, more radical than the metamorphosis of the caterpillar into a beautiful butterfly. God transforms the sinful heart of a man or woman into the image of His son, Jesus Christ. We cannot "reform" ourselves. We cannot "recover" what we never were. We can only ask God to perform His own heart surgery. David prayed in Psalm 51:10, **"Create in me a clean heart, O God, and renew a right spirit within me."**

God leaves some of our old habits in our newly transformed life. That is why we must continually pray and ask Him to show us our remaining sin, how to put-off our old selves, be renewed in the spirit, or attitude, of our minds, and to put-on our new selves, which is to be like Christ (Ephesians 4:22-24). The residue of indwelling sin is contained in our old habits of the flesh which affect us in three areas: thinking, speaking, and acting. In time and by His grace, God will transform those old habits, too, and replace them with godly ones that think, speak, and act righteously like Christ. God does this by giving you the power to replace your habitual, ungodly thoughts, words, and actions with godly ones that become automatic, or habitual, and seemingly unconscious. In this way, godliness can be learned and practiced just as a child learns by practicing the piano, hitting a baseball, or praying daily.

The heart must be transformed by the power of Christ first before the disciplined process of transformation can really begin. In Christianity, we think of transformation in two ways: justification (or salvation) and sanctification (or spiritual growth after salvation). The genuineness of the heart change of salvation will be most visible in the daily walk of spiritual growth, though, even for a Christian, there will be times when sin rears its ugly head. A Christian will daily face the war within: a battle between giving into the old habits of fleshly thinking, speaking, and acting versus walking in the Spirit (Ephesians 4 and 5) and newness of life.

At first, the Christian's new habits in the Spirit will not be very strong and will need to be developed through practice, or disciplined training in righteousness (2 Timothy 3:16). This is where the real work begins as a parent. Most parents fail by focusing only on the put-offs: "don't do this" or "stop doing that." Those are statements that parents make that rebuke the child but never train him in righteousness. I urge you as a parent to memorize and implement this key principle: focus on the put-on's for your child just as much as the put-off's. For example, teach your child what to say: "Don't say, 'Nah.' Instead, say 'No, thank you.'" Emphasize the right words to put-on and do not get weary if you must repeat your instructions continually.

In this way you will assist, encourage, and support your child in this process of biblical change. Ephesians 4:22-24 states **"to put off your old self, which belongs to your former manner of life and is corrupt through deceitful desires, [23] and to be renewed in the spirit of your minds, [24] and to put on the new self, created after the likeness of God in true righteousness and holiness."** Notice the importance of renewing the mind in the process of biblical change. When an "addict" is living selfishly according to the old person, the old mentalities must be addressed first in the transformation process. These five mentalities—the entitlement mentality, the consumer mentality, the victim, perishing, and rebellious mentalities will be addressed in the next chapters.

Conclusion

Transformation is both an instantaneous and an ongoing process. Both occur by God's grace. In the progressive process of transformation, your child is "partnering" with the Holy Spirit. This simply means that he is responsible for making every effort to fight sin and allow Christ to put-on righteousness, yet with the understanding that the He alone provides the willingness and power to carry out His commands by the Holy Spirit, according to Philippians 2:13: **"for it is God who works in you, both to will and to work for His good pleasure."**

This process of spiritual growth is life-long. Your child is 100% responsible for doing his part in the sanctification process and God is 100% sovereign and powerful to work in and through him in this same sanctification process. In that sense, it is a partnership between your child and Christ. The process involves the continual effort of putting off old thoughts, words, and behaviors and putting on new thoughts, words, and behaviors that are pleasing to God by renewing the mind (Ephesians 4:22-24). As a parent, you are responsible for directing your child in learning God's Word and in applying and living in the ways of the Lord according to Deuteronomy 6:7: **"You shall teach them diligently to your children, and shall talk of them when you sit in your house, and when you walk by the way, and when you lie down, and when you rise."**

KEY IDEAS AND PRACTICAL THINGS TO DO

1. Read and discuss Ephesians 4:21-24 with your child. Talk about the process of change in a Christian and how we are to put off old thoughts, words, and actions by replacing them with new thoughts, words, and actions.

2. Read and discuss Romans 12:1-2 with your child. Talk about how God wants us to be transformed by His power and not stuck coping with a lifelong problem that we never overcome.

3. Play the Put-off/Put-on Game with your child. For example, call out a thought, a word, or an action and ask your child if it is something we should put off or put-on (i.e. unrighteous or righteous). If it is a put-off, then ask your child what the opposite put-on alternative is that replaces it.

Chapter 10
Understanding Addictive Thinking

While their two buddies are in a fight outside, Derrick and Raymond are inside the house and back to smoking pot with some of their other friends. Derrick tells Raymond he doesn't like the way the Adderall ® makes him feel, but Raymond says he loves it and wishes he could take another pill or two. Raymond says he is going to see if he can go to the psychiatrist to get diagnosed with ADHD so that he can get a prescription for Adderall.®

What does addictive thinking look like and how can we identify it? An addict is living to please himself and to fulfill the desires of his own flesh. When I begin biblically counseling someone in active addiction, the five thought patterns or mentalities mentioned earlier are controlling his life. They are a mentality of entitlement, a consumer mentality, a victim mentality that gives birth to a perishing mentality, and finally a full-blown rebellious mentality. I call these "mentalities" because they are a predominant way of thinking about life. A "mentality" is defined as a "mode or way of thought" that affects one's outlook on life.[37] In subsequent chapters, we will go into more depth about the outlook of an "addict" and give you better insight into the thinking involved in active addiction.

What is interesting about these five mentalities is that each builds upon the previous one. First, parents, out of love, care for and nurture their infant child. In the beginning they mistakenly believe they must go to any lengths to keep little Ben happy, content, and certainly not crying. They determine, perhaps out of their own childhood experiences that little Ben will have everything in life they never had.

Ben likes this arrangement, and soon develops an "entitlement" mentality. He learns to become a "consumer" in our great society and life is good. When Ben begins to think that his entitlement needs and desires are not being met, he starts to develop a "victim" mentality. He thinks he deserves better than what he is receiving (entitlement)

---

[37] Merriam-Webster, I. (1996, c1993). *Merriam-Webster's Collegiate Dictionary.* Includes Index. (10th ed.). Springfield, Mass., U.S.A.: Merriam-Webster.

so he consumes whatever he has upon himself (consumer). When his parents do not grant his every desire, Ben begins to believe he is a victim of neglect or unfair treatment. His unmet desires frustrate him, but rather than blame himself, he blames others, his parents, perhaps his younger sibling, even God.

Now that Ben is thinking like a "victim," he will soon develop a "perishing mentality." This new mindset is mired in self-pity, focusing too much thought on himself in terms of what he does not have: "Bad things always happen to me." Psychologists have a different name for it as some call it a mild form of "learned helplessness." In reality, it often is a lack of gratitude that leads to despondent thinking, feeling sorry for oneself, and self-destructive actions. In the final stage, Ben, who now thinks with a "perishing mentality" begins thinking and acting like a rebel. He asks himself, "Why should I try to obey my parents or please them or please God?" The end result is a rebellious, angry, and foolish-acting child who wants to be independent—who seeks to be free from any rules, laws, or restrictions. The child wants to be his own boss at all costs.

What You Can Do

As a parent, you want to teach your child to think biblically so that he will not be prone to turn to addiction. Your child must **"be transformed by the renewal"** of his mind according to the Bible (Romans 12:2; Ephesians 4:23). In fact, we are all in need of transformed thinking so that we can discern the acceptable and perfect will of God. In other words, transformed thinking enables us to know what pleases God and benefits us when we actually put these things into practice.

As transforming Christians, everything hinges upon our thinking. In fact, as transforming Christians, we are all called to think, speak, and act in these five new, replacement "mentalities": humble, giving, responsible (also called obedient), grateful and submissive. Each of these mentalities is opposite of one of the five detrimental mentalities mentioned earlier. Here is a diagram to help you:

Put-off	Put-on
Entitlement	Be Humble
Consumer	Be Giving
Victim	Be Responsible (Obedient)
Perishing	Be Grateful
Rebellious	Be Submissive

Transformation begins in our mind. This whole process of transformation begins with Christ and His truth according to Ephesians 4:20-24: **"But that is not the way you learned Christ!— assuming that you have heard about him and were taught in him, as the truth is in Jesus, to put off your old self, which belongs to your former manner of life and is corrupt through deceitful desires, and to be renewed in the spirit of your minds, and to put on the new self, created after the likeness of God in true righteousness and holiness."** It all begins with the **"way you learned Christ...as the truth is in Jesus"** in verse 20. You and your child must learn about the true Jesus as He is presented in Scripture. Do not take someone else's idea about who they think Jesus is. You must study the Scriptures to learn about Him yourself! It is your relationship with Him that is important and not second-hand information. John 8:31-32 tells you: **"So Jesus said to the Jews who had believed in him, 'If you abide in my word, you are truly my disciples, and you will know the truth, and the truth will set you free.'"**

In Ephesians 4:23 above, the key for the put-off and put-on dynamic is provided: mind renewal. How is the mind renewed? Our minds are renewed by changing our thinking from being primarily concerned with pleasing ourselves to being concerned with pleasing God and others. Thoughts that are centered upon self must be replaced with God's Word of truth which will center our thoughts on Him and serving others. Again, everything hinges on changing our thinking, which is changing our beliefs! It is an act of faith in God and what He says rather than trusting our self.

Put-off	Renewing of the Mind	Put-on
Entitlement	The Word of God applied to thinking, emotions, & actions	Humility
Consumer	The Word of God applied to thinking, emotions, & actions	Giving
Victim	The Word of God applied to thinking, emotions, & actions	Responsibility (Obedient)
Perishing	The Word of God applied to thinking, emotions, & actions	Gratitude
Rebellious	The Word of God applied to thinking, emotions, & actions	Submission

You and your child must trust God at His Word. You must believe what the Bible says even when it contradicts your own feelings and experiences. For example, you may have been taught to trust your feelings but what if you feel like sinfully responding to a particular stimulus? Specifically, what if you get annoyed when your spouse buys himself a soft drink but does not think to buy one for you? You see how he is thoughtlessly enjoying his soft drink right in front of you, and it provokes you to such anger that you lash out at him with harsh, loud words that are sinful. Should you have trusted your feelings of anger? Or should you have realized that you were angry and handled the situation in a different way? Ephesians 4:26a says: **"Be angry and do not sin."** A loving thought would have been for you to think, "He must have been very thirsty, and he didn't think I might like a drink also. I will give him grace and not make him feel guilty."

Anger is an emotion that is produced by our thinking. Emotions and actions are always by-products of our thinking. Instead of thinking the worst about your spouse in this situation, you could have intentionally thought the best about him. 1 Corinthians 13:7 says that **"love bears all things, believes all things, hopes all things, endures all things."** Were you loving your spouse by believing the best about him in this situation or were you simply swept away by your emotion? Thinking is intentional. A person is responsible for his own thinking according to what Jesus said in Matthew 5:28: **"But I say to you that everyone who looks at a woman with lustful intent has already committed adultery with her in his heart."**

This example of thinking without acting out is akin to the actual commission of sin. Though the consequences would be different, the thought is still sinful in God's eyes because He alone sees the heart.

For this reason, addiction-proof parenting focuses upon helping your child to think biblically. It is the process of putting-off wrong thinking and putting-on right thinking. The first two mentalities called "entitlement" and "consumer" mentalities are opposite what is given in the Great Commandment in Matthew 22:37-40: **"And He said to him, 'You shall love the Lord your God with all your heart and with all your soul and with all your mind. This is the great and first commandment. And a second is like it: You shall love your neighbor as yourself. On these two commandments depend all the Law and the Prophets.'"** A child who is headed for an addictive lifestyle will be preoccupied with pleasing himself, thinking he is *entitled* to certain temporary pleasures of this world, and will *consume* those pleasures upon himself rather than giving them to help others. In Matthew 22:37 above, the Lord Jesus calls Christians to love God with our entire being which only comes when we see how lowly and undeserving we are and how great God is. This paradigm shift must occur first for your child to be addiction-proofed. Humility must replace an entitlement mentality.

The second mentality is "consumer" thinking and it is replaced when the child begins to think of others as much as he thinks of himself (v. 39): **"You shall love your neighbor as yourself."** Consider it in this way: what two-person relationship will not thrive when each person thinks of the other's needs and desires ahead of their own? A "consumer" mentality primarily thinks of what one can consume rather than what one can sacrifice and give to other people. A mindset of giving must replace a mindset of consuming. Parents must model how to "love your neighbor" in front of their children at home as well as with the actual "neighbor."

The last three detrimental *mentalities* that dominate the mind of the addict are the "victim" mentality, the "perishing" mentality, and the "rebellious" mentality. All three of these are replaced by the godly mindsets based upon Ephesians 5:18-21: **"And do not get drunk with wine, for that is debauchery, but be filled with the Spirit, addressing one another in psalms and hymns and spiritual songs, singing and making melody to the Lord with all your heart, giving thanks always and for everything to God the Father in the name of our Lord Jesus Christ, submitting to one another out of**

reverence for Christ." From this passage, a child must be taught to be responsible (obedient), grateful, and submissive. You may not be able to clearly discern these mentalities now, but by the end of this book, and most importantly, by God's grace, they will be clear to you. Remember that each of these biblical mentalities (responsibility, gratitude, and submission) is an exact antidote for the detrimental, "addictive" mentalities (victim, perishing, and rebellious).

Not Rocket Science

When I counsel someone trapped in active addiction and they want to begin living free of drugs, I work to help the person change their thinking by first addressing these three mentalities. I want to see humility, giving, responsibility, gratitude, and submission manifest abundantly in every facet of the counselee's life. In addition, I look for the motives and heart attitudes behind these mentalities because a proper motivation to glorify Christ is paramount. A counselee in the process of transformation will produce fruit in accordance with these five mentalities if their heart has truly been changed by Christ.

You as parents can work on all five of these areas daily to instill this way of thinking in your children. It is never too late for a child to learn to be responsible/obedient, grateful, and submissive to authorities. Even if he is not yet a believer in Christ, he must learn to think in these five new mentalities. If you fail to parent your children and leave them to go their own way, they will naturally gravitate toward the mentalities of feeling entitled, consuming things for temporary pleasure, thinking that they're a victim, having a perishing outlook, and thinking like a rebel. Children do not have to be taught to think selfishly like a perishing victim, or a rebel. But they *must be taught* how to think unselfishly, be humble, practice giving to others, be responsible, grateful for God's blessings, and submissive to authority. This responsibility for training through discipline belongs to parents.

Fake Fruit

In the chapters to follow, you will learn parenting strategies to help your children begin thinking biblically in these five primary areas. Here is where "the rubber meets the road" for a Christian. Our heart motives must be for the glory of God alone. 1 Corinthians 10:31 states: **"So whether you eat or drink, or whatever you do, do**

all to the glory of God." Train your child to become responsible, grateful, and submissive for the right reason: God's glory. That really is the primary reason. The benefit to parents and others is important but it is only a secondary reason. God must always come first.

Let me give you an example of some wrong heart motives behind humility, giving, responsibility, gratitude, and submission. These wrong heart motives are like the "fake fruit" that people sometimes put on their kitchen tables. It looks like real fruit from afar, but when you get close to it and reach for a grape and an apple, you realize it is not real fruit. Close examination reveals the truth. As Christians, we are not to judge others, but we can be "fruit inspectors." Take note that as you teach these lessons to your children, they will be inspecting your fruit as well. You must be what you want your children to be.

An example of false humility is taking pride in showing generosity only to be noticed by others. Pretending to be submissive when you know you are planning to have your own way is not only "fake fruit," but also sinful rebellion. Demonstrating responsibility only for selfish gain and manipulative gratitude are also examples of "fake fruit."

False humility, pride in showing generosity only to be noticed by others, demonstrating responsibility only for selfish gain, and manipulative gratitude are all examples of "fake fruit." The Holy Spirit utilizes the Word of God to bring about a renewal of the mind, heart, and soul of an individual. Internal, spiritual heart change is the only goal that is worth pursuing and only God has the power to exact heart change!

Conclusion

As a parent, you must utilize the Word of God often in your daily parental interactions with your children. Do not be afraid. You may feel inadequate to teach biblical principles to your children. Just remember that you need only be one step ahead of your child. If you are studying a small portion of Scripture, do your best to pull out the key ideas in that passage and teach them to your child. You do not have to memorize the entire Bible, although scripture memorization will prove to be a great aide to you in parenting. However, you do have to increase your knowledge of the Scriptures and use them in order for the Holy Spirit to help you apply them.

Appendix B will focus upon helping you and your child develop in three areas of the Bible: knowledge, understanding, and wisdom. As a parent, do not be satisfied with behavioral change but seek after and pray for genuine heart change, which only the Lord can bring. We are not powerful enough to control our children's hearts. Trust the Lord to change your child's heart. That will be an act of faith on your part. Whether you have a two-year-old, a teenager, or a twenty-two-year-old, these practical strategies will enable you to do the difficult yet rewarding work of addiction-proof parenting. By God's grace, He will bring real heart change in your child and in you!

KEY IDEAS AND PRACTICAL THINGS TO DO

1. Write out 1 Corinthians 13:4-7 and identify ways to love others, matching actions to each of the words identified in this passage of Scripture. Do this activity with your child's input.

2. Play the Put-off/Put-on Game with your child. This time, call out only thoughts and words that are put-offs (e.g., unrighteous) and ask your child what the likely action would be in response to it.

   A good resource for this game is *Transformed into His Likeness* by Armand Tiffe. (Focus Publishing, www.focuspublishing.com). It contains a list of 106 sins to put off with the coordinating list of biblical qualities to put on, as well as a list of Scripture for each quality. The format of this booklet is easy enough for children to use.

3. Read Appendix B and use it to begin teaching your child about God's Word. Go slowly and make small goals in the beginning. Start with memorizing the names of the books of the Bible in order.

Chapter 11
How to Raise an "Addict"

Before long, Derrick tells Raymond that his chest is really hurting. "Maybe I shouldn't have taken those Adderall," Derrick says. "I feel terrible." Raymond blows off Derrick's comment by saying, "Don't be a big baby." Derrick walks away from Raymond and is beginning to stumble. Falling to the floor, Derrick lands on his face as one of the girls at the party screams. Someone calls 911 and the paramedics are en route.

Let's pretend for a moment that you don't care if your child is raised as an "addict." What mistakes would you make as a parent to foster your child's "addictive," idolatrous thinking, speaking, and acting? C.S. Lewis wrote a book called *The Screwtape Letters* in which he depicted an older demon training a younger demon to deceive and torment God's children by feeding their fleshly desires. This book portrays how devious the enemy is in tempting us with lies that we want to believe. This chapter was written in like manner because I want you to see how deceptive cultural parenting can be— that it promotes flesh-feeding lies that Satan uses to tempt us.

My goal in this chapter is to provide an overview of the five basic mentalities of "addictive" thinking. Before presenting an in-depth description of each of the mentalities of idolaters and "addicts," this chapter will help you to see the mindset behind the poor parenting that feeds these dangerous mentalities. They are dangerous mindsets for children to have and will likely lead to "addictive" choices and behavior. For now, let this be an introduction to these concepts and then you may want to refer back to these lists after you finish the book. Now, in the spirit of C.S. Lewis' *The Screwtape Letters*, here is a list of several things you must be sure to do to ensure your child (or grandchild) becomes self-centered and "addicted" to something:

Parenting in General

- Spend more time on your computer than interacting with your child about meaningful topics.
- Spend more time doing anything for temporal gain than talking to, teaching, and listening to your child about meaningful, spiritual things.

- Never hug your child.
- Never re-assure your child of your unconditional love.
- Encourage your child to earn your love by doing tasks for you.
- Be a fake: tell your child one thing and do another.
- Lie to your child often.
- Use an angry, loud tone of voice with your child to get him to obey.
- Do not use the rod and reproof with your child, but yell at your child since verbal abuse is far better than what you believe to be "physical abuse."
- Demonstrate your anger with a loud tone of voice and physical violence.
- Give your child as many choices as you possibly can in one day.
- Give your child as much power to make decisions as early as you can—after all you won't always be his parent.
- Reinforce the notion that your child can only trust in himself and not in God or others.
- Model a trust in yourself; he needs to trust you right now, rather than in God.
- Never talk about God with your child—let the youth pastor or someone else do that. You don't want to look like a hypocrite.
- Do not pray before meals to give thanks to God, your Provider. After all, you alone are the provider for this family and they need to know it.
- Do not force your child to read the Bible, especially if they find it boring or difficult to understand.[38] It will only cause questioning and confusion that you are unable to answer.
- Do not force your child to do anything he deems unpleasant (i.e. washing dishes, taking out the garbage, sitting at home reading a book, etc.).

---

[38] Obviously, I am being sarcastic by calling the Bible "boring" and "difficult to understand." Have your child read Proverbs, Psalms, and other books of the Bible and you may be surprised at how well they understand it.

- Rather than be a proactive parent, be a reactive parent who only responds to problems rather than teaching the child what to do correctly. Certainly don't suggest possible problems or conflict in his future; you don't want to give him any negative ideas.

Entitlement Mentality

- Make your child believe that he is the center of the universe. Give in to his every whim and desire so that he knows the world revolves around him. Feed the "entitlement" mentality. It will help his self-esteem.
- Teach your child that the kingdom of God is not all about the King but it is all about your child. In other words, the kingdom exists for your child's pleasure, not for the King to be glorified.
- Fully inform your child of his "rights." Don't teach him that most things are privileges. No, they are his "rights." For example, make sure he has a right to drive a car at age 16, and be certain that it is a brand new car, with paid-for insurance, and the freedom to drive wherever he wishes because you certainly do not want your child to be different from his peers.
- Prevent all negative consequences in your child's life, especially when he has made a terrible choice. For example, if your child is disruptive in class and is suspended from school, be sure to complain to the principal and teachers loudly that you believe this is unfair treatment and that your child is being singled out for punishment.
- Do not allow your child to experience negative consequences from his wrong choices because that would be "embarrassing" to him and to you.
- Teach your child that self-worth comes from the things of this world rather than from a relationship with Christ.
- Feed your child's sense of entitlement by telling him he has a "right" to things. Allow him to "throw a temper tantrum" whenever he does not receive what "ought" to belong to him. (This creates resentments, too.)

Consumer Mentality

- Teach your child that he is a consumer who will find *eternal* satisfaction in the things of this *temporal* world. Feed the "consumer" mentality.
- Give everything to your child in abundance so that he will never go "without."
- Promote comfort at all costs. After all, isn't comfort the environment in which we grow best?
- Teach your child to focus on earthly things and the pleasures of this world as goals to be achieved rather than upon heavenward goals. For example, teach him to focus on seeking pleasure and avoiding all types of pain.
- Alleviate all pain medicinally and with comfort foods (or other temporary pleasures) so that your child never has to experience any pain or disappointment whatsoever in a fallen, sin-cursed, and selfish world.
- Teach your child to depend upon medicine (and other temporary pleasures) rather than upon God to alleviate pain.
- Do not talk about sin or a fallen world cursed by man's sinful choice to disobey God. Let your child wonder why there is death, sorrow, suffering, and pain in this world. That way, your child will blame God and not man for the sorrows, pain, and grief of this world.

Victim Mentality

- Allow your child to become irresponsible by providing no work, no chores, no rules, no discipline, no structure, no expectations, and no consequences for their actions. The school is much too strict anyway, and there's too much homework assigned.
- Excuse bad choices made by your child by saying, "It wasn't your fault," to create a "victim" mentality.
- Blame your child's environment for his wrong choices.
- Blame your child's other parent (not you) for his poor choices.

- Blame DNA and genetics for your child's poor choices.
- Blame yourself for your child's wrong choices.
- Never talk about your child's sin; only talk about grace without sin.
- Do not present the Gospel to your child.
- If you do present the Gospel to your child, then ignore the ugly "sin" part and only focus on God's grace. He loves us all anyway.
- Never point your child to confession and repentance of sin with Christ.
- Do not teach your child to pray and call out to God for forgiveness.
- Do not encourage your child to read the Bible; rather, allow him to play hours and hours of videogames (or some type of activity) while he still can. There is plenty of time for that other stuff; they are only children for such a short time.

Perishing Mentality

- Model ungratefulness before your child. After all, there is always something to gripe about in this rotten world.
- Always point out the bad in any situation that may appear to be good at first. Do not teach your child to be thankful for undesirable circumstances
- Make sure you tell your child early and often how this world always gives you a bad deal and how your family has always been dealt a bad hand in terms of money, opportunity, employment or education. Foster the "perishing" mentality of being mired in ungratefulness and self-pity.
- Do not teach your child to have a joyful mentality but to focus all thinking on what one does not have. That is the only way to motivate him to do better than all those before him.

Rebellious Mentality

- Teach your child to be self-reliant. He should know he can't count on anyone but himself.

- Teach him to be independent and self-sufficient and never to ask for help. Once you ask someone for help, they will want something from you later.

- Teach your child to trust in himself and never let him read or follow Proverbs 3:5-6.

- Arrange your schedule and your family's schedule around your child's sports schedule. In this way you can have a child-centered home.

- Put your child ahead of your spouse. The child is more important.

- Tell your child everything about all your relationships, even adult relationships. You certainly don't want to be accused of hiding things from your child. That way he will learn and be ready to make adult decisions.

- Do not teach your child manners or respect for others. It is old-fashioned and not important anymore. Actually, most adults don't deserve respect.

- Teach your child to be dishonoring to those who are older (i.e. senior adults).

- Control everything your child says and does. Answer any and all questions directed at your child, and make all decisions for him. Give your child too little freedom so he feels controlled in everything. Or,

- Allow your child to make all his decisions about food, clothing, choices of friends, future goals. You don't want to control him.

- Let your child decide if he wants to go to church or not.

- Choose a church based only upon what's best for your child.

- Foster high self-esteem in your child so that he thinks that he is the cause of all of his successes in life rather than the Lord.

- Teach your child to ignore the glory of God and to glory in self.

- Promote the glory and importance of positions and power rather than humble submission to God.
- Teach your child that there is no God or higher being and that he is totally in charge of his life and choices. And then really give them that control.
- Find your life's fulfillment in your child's sport activities. After all they did inherit your genetics, right? Model the importance of sports before them.
- Make your child the center of your universe.
- Do anything for your child (also called "enabling"), especially if you know it will avoid an unpleasant situation for them.
- Worship (think about, rely on, seek pleasure and joy from) your child rather than God.

Again, do not do the things listed in this chapter! They are lies. Perhaps some of you have recognized many of these mentalities as mistakes you have already made. Be encouraged! It is not too late. Remember that the above statements reinforce the flesh's desires in your child's sinful nature. When you read some of these statements, you may not see anything wrong with them at first glance. Parents must overcome their own sinful thinking before they can teach their children to recognize sin in their own lives.

Conclusion

Addiction-proof parenting can be exhausting, but I want to encourage you. It can only be done by God's grace. He is faithful to work in us and through us by the Holy Spirit to bring about a change in our thinking to be more biblical and Christ-like. When you begin to implement change as a parent, your child will respond to your lead and model you. I urge you not to take a single day off from being intentional with your child. Do not allow him to revert back to his primary nature of self-centeredness. Seek God and He will be found. Read His Word and ask for Him to illuminate it by the Holy Spirit. Then ask God to empower you to fulfill His will for your family for His glory. You must depend upon Him alone. Remember Proverbs 3:5-6!

KEY IDEAS AND PRACTICAL THINGS TO DO

1. Make and analyze a list of your top 10 priorities. Next to each one record the amount of time you spent on each activity during the past week. You may have to re-rank your priorities based upon the actual time you spent on each one to see what your priorities really were. This will show you what your priorities really were. Develop a plan to put your priorities in proper, biblical order.

2. Do you spend quality time or quantity time with your child? I recommend quantity time because it almost always produces quality as well. Be intentional by planning time each day to spend in a relaxing, calm environment where you read and discuss Bible passages with your child and pray together.

Section Three

Specific
Addiction-Proof
Parenting Principles

Chapter 12
The Entitlement Mentality

Edna, who is fifteen years old, takes the joint from one of her three girlfriends. She hurriedly walks outside to the front porch as they follow her. Edna pauses for a brief moment yet puts the joint to her mouth and inhales for a few seconds. Her friends giggle with glee as Edna smokes. However, their laughing stops abruptly when a set of bright lights shines in their eyes and a man's voice shouts, "Stop right there, young ladies. I'm Detective Smith with the police department. You are under arrest."

"It's all about me!" thinks the one-year old. "Mine, it's all mine!" says the two-year old as he grabs a toy puzzle from his older brother. "Me, me, me!" is the teenager's mindset. No one has to teach a child to throw a selfish temper tantrum when he is told no and cannot get his own way. Children arrive pre-wired with selfishness ever since the fall of Adam and Eve in the Garden of Eden.

In this chapter, I will address the first detrimental mentality in children that often leads to addictive actions. This mentality is foundational because it reverses what should be our attitude about man and God. Living for God is an afterthought while living for self is most important. Sadly, many parents unintentionally encourage this way of thinking, which fuels "addictive" and idolatrous desires. It is called an entitlement mentality.

Again, I emphasize the word mentality because all addictive behavior hinges upon one's thinking. As mentioned previously, a mentality is defined as a "mode or way of thought" which affects one's outlook on life.[39] As a parent, you must teach your child to think biblically and critically of the world by using the Scriptures. Learning about the entitlement mentality of an addict is foundational to gaining valuable insights into the thinking involved in active addiction. Common ways that parents unwittingly encourage this problematic thinking pattern will be illustrated as well.

---

[39] Merriam-Webster, I. (1996, c1993). *Merriam-Webster's Collegiate Dictionary.* Includes Index. (10th ed.). Springfield, Mass., U.S.A.: Merriam-Webster.

The Great Commandment

The entitlement mentality is derived from what Jesus said in Matthew 22:37-38: **"And he said to him, 'You shall love the Lord your God with all your heart and with all your soul and with all your mind. This is the great and first commandment.'"** Basically, any type of "addiction" manifests when we do not love the Lord God with all of our heart, soul, and *mind*. In other words, a person in active "addiction" is primarily concerned with pleasing himself and not the Lord; all of his faculties (heart, soul, and mind) are wrapped up in self. There is no loving relationship with the Lord, since he is only involved in loving self. It is a one person relationship that omits God and others. This is true for any and all types of "addiction."

Now, the entitlement mentality is simply the opposite of obeying the words of Christ in Matthew 22:37-38. The entitlement mentality is characterized by thinking that one has *rights* to things that are really gifts or privileges given by God. For an adult, this thinking may be fed by the belief that he has worked hard to earn all that he has and is therefore justified in satisfying his every desire. A person in this type of mindset thinks he deserves more than what he is getting. "I deserve better" and "I deserved that but I did not get it" is often what a person in this mode of thinking says to himself. "Addicts" who have this mentality wrongly think that the things of this earth exist to satisfy and please them. It is a self-centered, rather than a Christ-centered way of thinking. The earth and all that is in it belongs to the Lord; therefore, we are to serve the Lord who is the King of Kings.

Is It Worth It?

A story I heard in graduate school illustrates the entitlement mentality. A group of children were playing baseball in an empty field next door to a man's house. The field was not owned by the man but he was annoyed when children were playing loudly each day after school. Finally, the man devised a plan. He decided to offer them money. He met with the children and said, "Guys, I'm going to pay each of you every day for playing baseball in this field next to my house. After you finish playing, come over to my house and I'll give each of you a dollar." Every day after playing baseball, the children went next door and the man honored his word and gave them each a dollar.

After two weeks, the man met with the children again and said, "Guys, times are tough and I've got to cut back the dollar each day to 50 cents." For a week, the man honored his word and paid each child 50 cents for playing in the lot. The next week, the man told the children he had to lower his pay again to 25 cents. Each of the three weeks following, the man told the children he had to lower their pay to 10 cents, 5 cents, and then to a single penny.

When the children earned their first penny, they looked at the copper coin in their hands and said, "Hey, Mister, we are not going to play here for you anymore. It's not *worth* it." And the children never came back to play again.

Needless to say, the man in our story was very happy with the outcome. The children left because it was not "worth it" to play at the lot if the pay was too little. They had forgotten that they once played there for free and for fun. It took several weeks but the man succeeded in getting the children to stop playing baseball next to his house. The lesson for parents is that children will often play or do chores without any reward or motivation attached. Sometimes when you attach a value to something they do, they will become embittered when that benefit is not given. Parents often are their own worst enemies when it comes to creating an "entitlement mentality" and this mentality can contribute to ungrateful thinking.

Parents foster this attitude in their children by giving them everything they want. For example, in the grocery store, a child is going to see something he desires. "I want that toy, Mommy" or "I want that candy, Daddy" are common phrases spoken by children when they see something at the store. Parents cannot give in to a child's every whim and must learn to say "no." As parents, we want to please our children but giving them what they want every time they want it is not what is best for them. In fact, giving the child whatever he wants feeds the entitlement mentality because he begins to expect all of his desires to be met every time he cries out to his parent.

Children can develop excessive and unrealistic expectations. These expectations motivate them to ask for things and then to demand more things as they grow older. When these expectations are not met, the sad result is that they learn to respond with disappointment and anger, and then they try to manipulate the parent to get the desired thing. Resentments build up when expectations are unmet and these resentments often lead to selfish, "addictive" choices and behaviors.

I cannot emphasize this point enough. A parent who fosters an entitlement mentality in their child will inevitably provoke him to hurt, anger, resentment, bitterness, and stubbornness. A child is pre-wired to think this way if a parent allows it, and parents often encourage this thinking in their children by raising their child's expectations or trying to satisfy their every desire.

Another aspect of entitlement thinking is the idea that a child should not be expected to do chores around the house without being paid in some way. Parents often give their children a weekly allowance and in so doing outline what is expected for those monies. This is, in fact, a good way for children to learn how to handle money. They should be taught to tithe a portion, save a portion, and then to be good stewards of the rest. Be cautious about offering to pay them for chores around the house that should constitute their contribution to the work involved in running the household. Again, your child is not "entitled" to have mom or dad do everything to make his life comfortable.

Parents must teach their children that they are not to be self-centered but Christ-centered. Children are to desire what God desires. They are to want what God wants. Little children can be taught to think like this but it will take lots of effort by the parents. For example, a parent must teach the child that the toy they desire from the grocery store is only temporarily satisfying and that the greater goal is for eternal things. The child can be told that the money not spent on the toy is going to be spent on food for the family or, better yet, the money will be given to a charity to help children who have no food. There is no need to hide the real needs of others from your children as many children in third world countries do not have food, shelter, clothing, shoes, and running water!

Distinguish between "needs" and "desires" for your child. For example, if a child says, "Mommy, I need that toy" you must clarify the comment and re-state it for him: "You do not need the toy. You do have a desire to play with the toy. A need is food, water, clothing, and shelter. Toys are a desire, my child." Check your own language to be sure you use these words correctly, too. Many parents teach their children wrongly that desires, wants, and preferences are "needs" when they are not. This is a distinction you as parents must understand as you evaluate your own "needs" and "desires."

Too many people make the desires of their heart a "need," and then when that so-called need goes unmet, it becomes the center of their universe. Be sure you use the words "needs" and "desires" correctly with your children to avoid confusion and wrong expectations. Don't hesitate to review the true definition of "needs" with your children when you hear them say, "I need that—." It will be good for them to know the distinction.

Do not feed the flesh of your child, who will naturally desire all kinds of things of this temporary world. Instead, foster an eternal mindset to desire spiritual things like love, joy, peace, patience, kindness, goodness, faithfulness, gentleness, and self-control (Galatians 5:22-23).

I often ask audiences this question: what two things in this room will live forever? The correct answer is not always given. The correct answer is only the souls of those in the room and the Word of God. Everything else in that room will burn up at the end of time; therefore, intentionally teach your child to have an eternal perspective rather than a temporal one and to focus upon things that will last forever. Souls are most important and your child's soul is to be taught—to be led to Christ to live forever with Him. Teach your child that he is a living soul, living in an earthly body that will decay and die. Eventually, God will resurrect His children and give them renewed bodies that will never perish (1 Corinthians 15:50-58). Teach your child to set his mind on things above rather than on things below (Colossians 3:2).

Conclusion

An entitlement mentality actually cheapens the worth of God and other people while falsely elevating our own worth. What a lie! This mentality encourages us to think too highly of ourselves, which, in turn, encourages thinking too lowly of others and of God. "The world does not revolve around you" is a phrase heard when someone is being confronted for thinking too selfishly. A child who is allowed to think that the world is "all about me" will not understand his/her place in this world and will become angry and frustrated with the multitude of disappointments a fallen world produces. Development of some kind of addiction is only a matter of time for a child who thinks of himself as entitled to the things of this life. Remember James 4:6, that **"God opposes the proud, but gives grace to the humble."** Don't you want the grace of God in the lives of your children? If so, teach them to think more highly of God and others than they think of themselves.

KEY IDEAS AND PRACTICAL THINGS TO DO

1. Read Genesis chapters 1-3 with your child and discuss being created in the image of God, the fall of sin, and living in a fallen world until the return of Christ. Teach your child to be mindful that God created him and not the other way around.

2. List several ways that the Lord has blessed you and your child though you did not deserve it.

3. Go to a nursing home or children's hospital where you and your child will see people less fortunate than you. Take them gifts and spend time talking with them to hear their stories. Serve them by listening to them.

4. BONUS: Do NOT use the word "need" but substitute the word "desire" in its place for a month. If you do slip and use the word incorrectly, quickly call attention to yourself and then recite the four basic needs: food, water, clothing and shelter.

Chapter 13
Be Humble

It takes several guys to break up the fight between Freddie, Matt, and the two other guys. Freddie has a bloody nose and Matt is holding his right arm. Both boys look badly beaten with bruises, cuts, rips in their clothing, and blood smeared on their faces. In the background, Freddie hears a siren and panics. His only words are "Oh, no!" as he briskly walks toward the front porch of his house where he suddenly sees flashing blue lights and the police holding Edna by the arm.

The replacement for an entitlement mentality is humility. It is your parental responsibility to teach your child to have a humble mindset rather than an entitlement mentality. Humility is a virtue that does not occur naturally. It must be taught, and when you think you've attained humility, it is at that point you should know you have not. It is like the pastor whose congregation presented him with a button that said, "World's Most Humble Preacher," and when he wore it, they took it away from him.

Philippians 2:5-11 draws attention to our Lord Jesus Christ who humbled Himself willingly to be an example for you and your child:

> **Have this mind among yourselves, which is yours in Christ Jesus, who, though he was in the form of God, did not count equality with God a thing to be grasped, but made himself nothing, taking the form of a servant, being born in the likeness of men. And being found in human form, he humbled himself by becoming obedient to the point of death, even death on a cross. Therefore God has highly exalted him and bestowed on him the name that is above every name, so that at the name of Jesus every knee should bow, in heaven and on earth and under the earth, and every tongue confess that Jesus Christ is Lord, to the glory of God the Father.**

Humility is a counter-cultural concept in today's society. If anything, American thinking encourages pride and frowns upon humility. Our culture wrongly sees humility as weakness rather than meekness. Meekness is power under the control of the Holy Spirit. The meekest man next to Jesus was Moses, who was fearful that his speech impediment would hinder his call by God to lead the people of Israel. Moses' focus was not on the Lord but on his own inadequacies. In fact, Moses' lack of faith in God (caused by his wrong focus upon himself) made the Lord angry as recorded in Exodus 4:10-17:

> But Moses said to the LORD, "Oh, my Lord, I am not eloquent, either in the past or since you have spoken to your servant, but I am slow of speech and of tongue." Then the LORD said to him, "Who has made man's mouth? Who makes him mute, or deaf, or seeing, or blind? Is it not I, the LORD? Now therefore go, and I will be with your mouth and teach you what you shall speak." But he said, "Oh, my Lord, please send someone else." Then the anger of the LORD was kindled against Moses and he said, "Is there not Aaron, your brother, the Levite? I know that he can speak well. Behold, he is coming out to meet you, and when he sees you, he will be glad in his heart. You shall speak to him and put the words in his mouth, and I will be with your mouth and with his mouth and will teach you both what to do. He shall speak for you to the people, and he shall be your mouth, and you shall be as God to him. And take in your hand this staff, with which you shall do the signs.

In His displeasure with Moses, God was still gracious to him by providing Aaron to assist him in his area of weakness. God is gracious even when He is angry because He alone is love. It is fine to admit you have weaknesses as a parent, with the daunting task of raising godly children, but God's power and grace are what is needed to do the job and He is faithful. Any lack of faith you have in Him stems from fear and doubt rather than trust in the Lord.

Fostering Humility in Your Child

Few people know what true humility looks like. It is best defined as "the mindset of Christ (a servant's mindset); a focus on God and others, a pursuit of the recognition and the exaltation of God, and a desire to glorify and please God in all things and by all things He has given."[40] Humility is unnatural to our flesh, as it is only produced and expressed in a Christian by the Holy Spirit. It is a foreign concept to children and must be taught. Unless we are transformed in our thinking, our humility will lead us to pride and a high opinion of our own sanctity.

In his excellent booklet on humility, Dr. Stuart Scott lists 24 manifestations of humility and 24 manifestations of pride. He uses the Scriptures to tell us what humility looks like in a Christian's life. Here are some that your children can learn early in life:

- Recognizing and trusting God's character (Psalm 119:66)
- Seeing yourself as having no right to question or judge an Almighty and Perfect God (Psalm 145:17; Romans 9:19-23)
- Focusing on Christ (Philippians 1:21; Hebrews 12:1-2)
- Biblical praying and a great deal of it (1 Thessalonians 5:17; 1 Timothy 2:1-2)
- Being overwhelmed with God's undeserved grace and goodness (Psalm 116:12-19)
- Being thankful and grateful in general toward others (1 Thessalonians 5:18)
- Being gentle and patient (Colossians 3:12-14)
- Seeing yourself as no better than others (Romans 12:16; Ephesians 3:8)
- Having an accurate view of your gifts and abilities (Romans 12:3)
- Being a good listener (James 1:19; Philippians. 2:3-4)[41]
- Be thankful and grateful in general toward others. Humble people thank God and others often. (1 Thessalonians 5:18)
- Be gentle and patient. Humble people want to love others the way God loves them. (Colossians 3:12-14)
- See yourself as no better than others (Romans 12:16; Ephesians 3:8)

---

[40] Scott, Stuart, *From Pride to Humility*, Focus Publishing, Bemidji, MN, 2002, p. 18-21.
[41] Ibid, p. 18-19.

- Be a good listener (James 1:19; Philippians. 2:3-4)
- Talk about others only if it is good or for their own good. (Proverbs 11:13)
- Be gladly submissive and obedient to those in authority. (Romans 12:1-2; 13:1-2)
- Prefer others over yourself. (Romans 12:10)
- Be thankful for criticism or reproof. (Proverbs 9:8; 27:5-6)
- Be quick to admit when you are wrong. (Proverbs 29:23)
- Be genuinely glad for others. Humble people rejoice with others when good things happen to them (Romans 12:15).[42]

I strongly recommend that you purchase this booklet and study these attributes so you may learn how to be more Christ-like yourself and instill these qualities in your child. Those who struggle with any addiction often think that they are perfect and God is lacking. This is called pride and we know that the opposite is true: we are flawed and God alone is perfect. Humble Christians know this. Most important, humility must be modeled by the parent. No amount of instruction can substitute for a humble attitude on the part of those teaching it.

Despite Moses' weakness, God called him to lead Israel. In the natural world, it seems as if a pre-requisite for Moses' position of leadership would be clear speaking abilities. However, God used Moses' weakness to demonstrate His power. 1 Corinthians 1:27-29 states: **"But God chose what is foolish in the world to shame the wise; God chose what is weak in the world to shame the strong; God chose what is low and despised in the world, even things that are not, to bring to nothing things that are, so that no human being might boast in the presence of God."**

Train your children to give glory to God in all things. 1 Corinthians 10:31 states: **"So, whether you eat or drink, or whatever you do, do all to the glory of God."** Can it be any clearer? Do everything to the glory of God, not yourself. While you want your children to be familiar with their own strengths and abilities, you must teach them to humbly acknowledge God as the Giver of those strengths and abilities.

Did you ever wonder why God wants glory? I believe one reason

---

[42] Ibid, p. 18-21

is because glorifying Him brings people to their knees to see Him for who He really is—a perfect Father, full of loving-kindness toward mankind. Seeing God's glory magnifies Him in our eyes. God already is huge and the whole earth is full of His glory, but we sometimes miss seeing that truth because our focus is upon ourselves.

Does God deserve glory? Yes, in fact, God alone deserves glory. He alone is worthy to be praised. He will not share His glory with any created being, your child included. In a quick sentence, God wants us to "get over ourselves" and to revel in Him. We are created, needy, dependent, and weak people who need God and others in order to survive. A baby must have someone to provide care, food, and shelter for him. A baby is dependent upon others. In reality, for our entire lives, we are dependent upon God and others.

Likewise, you want your child to be mindful of his weaknesses and inabilities so you can use these things to draw his eyes to look to God to work through him to fulfill his calling, as He did through Moses. You do not want your child to be consumed with his weaknesses, just aware of them so he depends, trusts, and relies upon God for all things. God calls fearful people to faithful ministries. God calls humble people to serve Him in mighty ways. God wants the glory and He deserves it.

Conclusion

Addiction-proof parenting must be grounded in a foundation of humility. Humility is a mindset that is cultivated over a lifetime. None of us have perfected humility because we are prone to be prideful and trusting in ourselves (Proverbs 3:5-8). God uses our pride to humble us when things do not happen according to our plans. Then He uses that humility to build our confidence in Him.

Humility finds power in Christ, and not in self. Humility encourages prayer to God who alone has all power. Humility is the mindset of a servant and steward of God's grace and mercy. When your children recognize their great need for Christ and that their loving Heavenly Father can be greatly depended upon to meet that need, they will be saved for all of eternity. Humble reliance upon God is a pre-requisite for addiction-proof parenting and it must be instilled in your child since it does not happen naturally.

KEY IDEAS AND PRACTICAL THINGS TO DO

1. Read about Moses' life in the book of Exodus and how the Lord mightily used this humble, meek man for the Lord's glory.

2. Refer to Dr. Stuart Scott's list given on pages 18-21 of his booklet. Read each Scripture reference. Write out practical ways that you can exhibit more humility in each area.

3. Write out Proverbs 3:5-8 on a sheet of paper or 3x5 cards. List ways you have trusted the Lord in your past and been blessed. List ways you have trusted in yourself in the past and it led to disappointment and suffering. Share these with your children as part of your testimony of His faithfulness despite your unfaithfulness at times.

Chapter 14
The Consumer Mentality

The paramedics pull up to the front of the house and are directed to Derrick who is lying unconscious on the living room floor. They begin CPR and moments later decide to take Derrick to the hospital. Raymond, Freddie, Matt, and the others watch as Derrick remains unconscious and is loaded into the ambulance.

We live in a consumer society. Children and teen-agers have more discretionary spending than ever before in history. Large corporations study the spending trends of children and promote their products aggressively on television and in magazines. Birthdays and Christmas are celebrated with excessive and often extravagant piles of gifts, toys and clothing that will be discarded as soon as the next craze comes along.

This describes the second mentality that parents foster in their children. It is the consumer mentality. Similar to the entitlement mentality in several ways, a consumer is someone who "destroys, spends wastefully, squanders, and uses up" things.[43] To consume a product is to use it fully. A fire that consumes a house burns it down to the ground completely. A child who is a consumer uses everything to its fullest extent, including people!

Those who possess a consumer mentality do not think with a grateful heart. Their desire is to spend all of their resources upon their own selfish pursuits rather than to help others. This consumer mentality is based upon a failure to follow the second part of the Great Commandment in Matthew 22:39: **"And a second is like it: You shall love your neighbor as yourself."** A "neighbor" in this verse means "near one." Sometimes when we read that verse we think of a next door neighbor who lives beside us. However, a "neighbor" is best understood to be a "near one" meaning someone who is near in our everyday life. Examples of "near ones" include family members, colleagues at work, other students at school, friends, and people you see regularly at the grocery store.

---

[43] Merriam-Webster, I. (1996, c1993). *Merriam-Webster's Collegiate Dictionary.* Includes Index, (10th Ed.). Springfield, Mass., U.S.A.: Merriam-Webster.

So how should we love our near ones? One way is by giving of our time, talents, and treasures to help others in need. Being a blessing to others is a crucial component of the committed Christian walk. However, the "consumer" is primarily concerned with pleasing one person: self. Therefore, their time, talents, and treasures are wrongly spent for selfish pursuits without consideration of others. For example, money may be spent on an "addictive" shopping spree for enjoyment rather than on the electric bill.[44]

A biblical example of a "consumer" is the prodigal son in Luke 15:11-32. This young man squandered his future inheritance on luxurious living and ended up in poverty. One biblical warning about being an excessive consumer is found in Proverbs 23:19-21: **"Hear, my son, and be wise, and direct your heart in the way. Be not among drunkards or among gluttonous eaters of meat, for the drunkard and the glutton will come to poverty, and slumber will clothe them with rags."** When a person has the mindset of an excessive consumer, it will ultimately lead to poverty. That is the natural consequence of this mindset because they will ultimately use up all of their resources. Pretty simple concept, really!

Please understand that being a consumer at times is not sinful. Moderation is the key. When you purchase an item like a car, you should utilize it for its intended purpose and see it as a blessing from God. The consumer mentality is detrimental when it is consumed with pleasing oneself excessively. The Lord wants us to be "givers" more than we are "takers." Acts 20:35 states it this way: **"In all things I have shown you that by working hard in this way we must help the weak and remember the words of the Lord Jesus, how he himself said, 'It is more blessed to give than to receive.'"** Because of a focus upon self and his own resources, the consumer does not see himself as blessed but as needy, so it's difficult for the consumer to think of giving to others more than receiving.

The consumer's self-centered mindset sees people and things as "objects" to be enjoyed, used for selfish reasons, and consumed. Many parents today are unaware that they are teaching their children to be consumers. Television and the United States economy depend upon consumerism; therefore, the world will reinforce this message

---

[44] Please understand the word "addictive" to describe a shopping spree is a worldly idea and the Bible would describe it as being a poor steward of God-given resources, or idolatry.

to your child in all varieties of commercials and news reports.

When I sit down to counsel a child and ask questions, I find that many who struggle with various "addictions" have a "consumer" mentality as well as a strong desire to escape by using up a consumer good. For example, the person who eats excessively (called an overeating "addiction" by the world) to deal with overpowering emotions such as hurt and anger will seek to change his reality using food. The consumption of food will temporarily delay the hurt and anger with a temporal pleasure, but that will only last until the next hunger or desire appears. The hurt or resentment does not magically go away but is "stuffed" down inside of the person. No healing occurs to deal with the hurt so nothing is resolved.

Parents often give their child a drink or a snack to change their emotional state of crying, whining, boredom, and the like. Although it may be unintentional, parents are sending the message that something outside of the child is what "fixes" and changes the child's emotional state. In this case it is food, but many times parents put a strong emphasis on medicine, television, video games, and the like to change the child's emotional state. While not necessarily intentional, the message from the parent to the child is clear and dangerous: "Something tangible outside of you will change your state of being or bad attitude."

While I agree that it is something outside of the child that is needed, I would emphasize that the "something" is spiritual and not a physical "fix." Hug your child to reassure him of your love. This may seem like an emotional fix but it reassures your child of the love of God, which is spiritual. The child must be taught not to be a consumer of physical, temporal pleasures but to be a worshiper of Christ. Christ is what the child really needs, so a parent must direct the child's eyes toward Him and not toward physical things. By directing the child toward Christ, I mean that the parent can teach the child that time spent in prayer with the Lord and reading His Word are productive things to do that are not consumer driven but instead keep their focus on God. The goal for parents will be to train their children to pray and study the Word as acts of worship, spiritual growth, and to help others.

Parents who allow or encourage their children to be ruled by emotions will fail at addiction-proof parenting. You must teach your child to be responsible by doing the right thing no matter how he feels. Allowing a child to make decisions that are led by emotion will only lead to an entitlement and consumer mentality. For example, it is always hurtful and discouraging for a child to discover he has not been invited to a friend's birthday party. It would be easy for you to try and compensate for your child's hurt by saying, "Why don't we go out for some ice cream and not even think about it." What is the message you are giving your child? Obviously, sweet treats will help us feel better when we are hurting.

Better still would be a biblical approach: "Honey, I know you are feeling left out by this, but your very best friend is Jesus who said He will <u>never</u> leave you or forsake you" (Hebrews 13:5). Teach your child to react to circumstances according to God's Word rather than according to his emotional state. Emotional decisions made out of hurt, anger, and fear likely lead to harder consequences rather than life-giving solutions. In this case, it would have been sinful to hold a grudge against the other child.

Likewise, as parents we should teach our children to see the difference between temporary pleasure and eternal joy. The birthday party above was a temporary pleasure. Discuss the difference between temporal and eternal pleasure with your child. Help them to see the bigger picture.

Sacrifice is the key mindset to counter a consumer mentality. A.B. Simpson once urged his organization, now called the Christian and Missionary Alliance, to give sacrificially to support missionaries in the work of the Great Commission in the effort to reach the world's lost people with the good news of the gospel. Financially speaking, Dr. Simpson said that you should give what you can, add more for faith, and then add more for sacrifice! Wow, that's a hard teaching but Dr. Simpson lived his life wholly committed to Christ.

"Addictive" mindsets tell us to avoid pain at all costs. Consumer mentalities foster addiction by feeding the desire to escape and avoid pain. In fact, the word "amusement" means "without thinking," and that's what consumers are doing: avoiding thinking by enjoying a temporary, mindless physical pleasure.

Teach your child to cherish spiritual pleasures like helping others. I often tell counselees in sessions the following: "This world is not meant to be our home. The temporary pleasures of this world are fleeting. In fact, the best physical pleasure this world can offer me is drinking a cola and having a nice meal. Those are temporary enjoyments for me, and that's the best it can ever be—

temporary. However, my biggest spiritual pleasure is spending time in discipleship and biblical counseling. Those pleasures for me are eternal and have a great impact both in this life and in the life to come!"

Parents accomplish this goal by helping their children to not think like consumers, but as responsible *stewards* who belong to Christ. God owns your child in the sense that He is your child's Creator. God is good and loving, so He best knows how you need to parent the child He has given you to shepherd. Point your child to Christ and His agenda.

Consider this aspect of the consumer mentality. Children who are consumers do not have an "investment" in the success of the family. For example, imagine you are shopping at your favorite grocery store. Suddenly, someone spills a drink on the floor. The manager runs up to you with a mop and says, "Here you go. Use this mop to clean up the spill for us. Thanks!" and walks away. You may stand there in disbelief, but then what are you going to do? Are you going to mop up the spill? Most likely you will think that as a consumer and patron of the store, you should not be expected to clean up the mess. You are there to buy a consumable good and leave. You have no investment there. It is absurd that they would ask you, a consumer, to clean up the store!

However, now imagine you are the owner of the store. As the owner, when you see a spill, you may be the first one to grab a mop to clean up the mess. Your attitude is different because owners have an investment and a stake in the success of their store. As an owner, you want to clean up the mess, but that's not the same attitude of a consumer or someone who thinks in the entitlement mentality. Can you begin to see how fulfilling the child's every whim is failing to teach the child to sacrifice, to serve others, and contribute to the success of the family?

As parents, do we need to serve our children? Yes. However, serving is teaching the child to serve God and others. Many church programs fall short because they seek to make consumers out of children and adults alike; God does not want His children to be spectators but participants in ministry.[45] The primary way to motivate

---

[45] My book, *Strength in Numbers,* is designed to move lay persons in the church from spectator to participant in the arena of discipleship and biblical counseling.

your children to think of others is by shifting their focus away from temporal pleasures and toward eternal productivity. Your child can be a vital part of the body of Christ, but only if you first teach him to think spiritually. Teaching the spiritual reality will, as a result, lead him to fulfillment in the physical reality.

Teach your child to fulfill his responsibilities in this life to avoid promoting both an entitlement and consumer mentality. The issue of responsibility is a difficult concept to explain to children because they are responsible for what God has given them; however, they are responsible as <u>stewards</u>, not as <u>owners</u>. Consumers think like owners and they mistakenly think they own their selves and their possessions, and they are, therefore, only responsible to themselves. This important concept comes into every area of life, from the toy your child received for his birthday, to your teenager's body that God desires him to keep sexually pure. You take care of what God has given you (toys or bodies) because ultimately they belong to Him. This requires an entire paradigm shift—a new way of thinking that comes from renewing your mind and your child's mind with biblical principles to teach him to say, "God is the Owner, I am only His steward and servant. As His steward, I will seek to honor Him."

Finally, please remember that we are souls first. Now we are souls housed in fallen, sin-stained bodies; however, one day we will be given a renewed, transformed body in the next life which will last for eternity. Our home is in that life and not in this life! Our mindset must be like that of Colossians 3:1-5:

> **If then you have been raised with Christ, seek the things that are above, where Christ is, seated at the right hand of God. Set your minds on things that are above, not on things that are on earth. For you have died, and your life is hidden with Christ in God. When Christ who is your life appears, then you also will appear with him in glory. Put to death therefore what is earthly in you: sexual immorality, impurity, passion, evil desire, and covetousness, which is idolatry.**

Conclusion

Both the consumer and entitlement mentalities are devastating outlooks for a child to have because they feed the flesh, promote "addictive" thinking and actions, and are concerned most with pleasing self rather than worshiping Christ by serving others. These mentalities are destructive because they focus only on the "here and now." Eternity is not in view when children and adults think like consumers and entitled persons, mistakenly thinking they deserve temporary pleasures to escape the pain of this world. Maybe the pain of this world is designed to motivate your child to appropriate action. That action might be to pray, share the gospel, help hurting souls, disciple Christians, and to study the Word of God to build up the body of Christ.

Our goal must not be to avoid pain and seek pleasure or to foster that type of attitude in our children. Teach your children to embrace the goal of worshiping God by serving others just as Jesus did. He came not to be served but to serve as He gave His life as a ransom for the salvation of many, according to Matthew 20:28. Likewise, you must have the mind of Christ and you must model and teach it to your child beginning at the youngest age possible! Colossians 3:12-17 tells you what the mind of Christ looks like so you can help your child to have His mind:

> **Put on then, as God's chosen ones, holy and beloved, compassion, kindness, humility, meekness, and patience, bearing with one another and, if one has a complaint against another, forgiving each other; as the Lord has forgiven you, so you also must forgive. And above all these put on love, which binds everything together in perfect harmony. And let the peace of Christ rule in your hearts, to which indeed you were called in one body. And be thankful. Let the word of Christ dwell in you richly, teaching and admonishing one another in all wisdom, singing psalms and hymns and spiritual songs, with thankfulness in your hearts to God. And whatever you do, in word or deed, do everything in the name of the Lord Jesus, giving thanks to God the Father through him.**

KEY IDEAS AND PRACTICAL THINGS TO DO

1. Each of you (child and adult alike) list 3 temporal things that you can bless someone else with by giving to them personally, or to a charity of your choice, or the like.

2. List several ways that you can live sacrificially in order to further the Lord's work in your church. For example, you may want to cancel cable television and send the extra money to missionaries. Be creative; no sacrifice is too small. Recall the widow Jesus saw and praised in Mark 12:42-44. If you cannot come up with any ideas, read how Jesus Christ gave His life on the cross in Matthew 26 & 27 and reconsider what you can give back to Him (Matthew 16:24).

3. Teach your child about the biblical principles of stewardship and ownership. Remind your child that God owns everything, including your child, and we are simply stewards of what He has temporarily entrusted to us.

Chapter 15
Be Giving

Derrick's mother is contacted by the police. When she arrives at the hospital, Derrick is already dead from cardiac arrest. He could not be revived. The toxic mix of large amounts of alcohol, marijuana, and Adderall were too much for his young body to handle. It was the most severe consequence a seventeen year old boy could experience from one night of so-called "partying" and "fun."

Consumers are "takers" and not "givers." "Takers" are never satisfied with what they consume and they want more and more and more and more. Those in active addiction are "takers" and "consumers." They have little thought of giving to others as most of their thoughts revolve around what they can get. Does this remind you of some children you know? This mentality leads to an ungrateful heart because the heart can never be satisfied with temporary pleasures. Only eternal treasures are satisfying.

Perhaps you have observed this by watching a child at Christmas or his birthday. There are so many gifts, and as each one is opened there is a brief expression of delight before the gift is tossed aside for another. Most disappointingly, watch his behavior when he reaches the bottom of the pile of gifts and still wants more.

Once we become Christians, our hearts will be filled with praise for the Lord. When that occurs, we worship Him by praying to Him, praising Him, and studying His Word. We return thanks to Him with grateful hearts for what He has done to redeem us from our sins. When God's grace and mercy overwhelm us we begin to love others more and desire to demonstrate God's love to them.

The replacement mentality for consumers is to have a giving heart. The very heart of God is to give to others. Those with a consumer mentality do not think grateful thoughts. Their desires are never satisfied; therefore, why would they ever be grateful? They must learn to be content just as the Apostle Paul said that he learned contentment, in Philippians 4:11: **"Not that I am speaking of being in need, for I have learned in whatever situation I am to be content."** He learned to be content when he had very little and when he had very much. His strength came from his relationship with the Lord and not from having the things of this world temporarily satisfy his desires.

This chapter on the topic of giving is important because being a blessing to others is a crucial component of the committed Christian walk. Often we find that an addict's life has been too easy. Many of those who are caught in active addiction are what the world would call "spoiled brats." They have been given everything and even believe they are entitled to that and more. Again, it is rooted in the entitlement and consumer mentalities. These children talk like entitled consumers with ungrateful hearts, saying things in an angry tone of voice, such as:

"Give me another piece of candy, Mommy."
"I want my toy now."
"No, you cannot have it. It's mine."
"Me. Me. Me." Or "Mine. Mine. Mine." You will often hear the words I, me, and mine from these children who are allowed to think selfishly in this manner.
"I deserve it, Daddy."
"It's not fair!"
"What about me, Mommy?" as the child observes his younger brother get a treat.

Again, giving your children everything they want simply fosters the consumer mentality. An example occurred when one of our children's friends attended a Sunday school class at our church. He was given an inexpensive, dollar store toy each week for coloring one work page and listening to the story. After a few weeks, the child began to expect a toy. When a substitute teacher taught the class one week, the child threw a temper tantrum expressing great displeasure that the toy was not given out that week. The toy had become an expectation rather than an infrequent reward. Many parents do this same type of thing with their children.

The truth is that children often do better with very little. They learn to play without many toys. Children do not need lots of stimulating toys to play and have fun. They figure out a way to have fun with whatever they have. Even a stick can be great fun to a young boy! As a parent, you may be fostering a consumer mentality in your child if you purchase something for them each time you go to the store. The child will grow to expect it and you will have raised your own greedy monster!

For this reason, teach your child to give. If he already likes to shop, teach him to shop with a heart for others. Model it before your child by saying, "This is what your grandmother would like to have. Let's get this for her!" Praise your child for thinking of others when you go shopping and encourage him to think about getting something for a particular relative by saying, "Let's look for a shirt for your cousin." Involve your child in that activity so he is a part of the process of buying and giving.

Teach your child the joy of giving a gift in secret. When you give a gift or do something special (an act of charity) for everyone to see, you have your reward here and now. People will notice and praise and thank you. But giving a gift in secret is a great blessing to you and the receiver of the gift (Matthew 6:2-4). Hint: Young children should be taught to check with Mom or Dad before they give things away in secret.)

Encourage your child to give to the church. Teach him to put a portion of what he has earned in the offering plate in order to cultivate the habit of giving. Also, giving to the church may mean giving your time and talents as well as financial gifts. Involve your child in a work project you can do together. Volunteer to clean a portion of your church's building or yard area simply to involve your child in that event. Your child will learn to be a giver by watching and modeling you!

Pray for pastors, church employees, missionaries, and those who are suffering for the sake of the Gospel. Teach your child to have a broken heart for the world by allowing him to go on mission trips through your local church when he is old enough. James 2:15-17 states: **"If a brother or sister is poorly clothed and lacking in daily food, and one of you says to them, 'Go in peace, be warmed and filled,' without giving them the things needed for the body, what good is that? So also faith by itself, if it does not have works, is dead."**

On holidays, instead of giving each other Christmas presents, go down to a soup kitchen to help feed those who are less fortunate. In our family, rather than give presents to their cousins (there are 22 cousins in all thus far) we ask our children and their cousins to put that money toward a worthy cause and we pick a different charity each year.

Overall, the idea is to help your child to be less self-focused and more focused upon the real needs of others. Think how rewarding it will be when he offers to give money toward a charity or to another person in need without being told to do so. It will happen in time but only if you teach your child to follow Matthew 22:39: **"You shall love your neighbor as yourself."**

Conclusion

As a parent, you must be intentional in teaching your child to follow the Great Commandment of Matthew 22:37-40. All God commands us to do is to love Him with our entire being and to love others as much as we already love ourselves. You can actually accomplish BOTH of these commandments (loving God and loving others) at the same time by giving to those in need. How about that for a double blessing!

KEY IDEAS AND PRACTICAL THINGS TO DO

1. Write out Matthew 22:37-40 and memorize it with your child.

2. List how you can give your time, talents, and treasures to others rather than spending them upon yourselves. Some churches participate in the Shoebox program with Samaritan's Purse. Your child will find joy in filling a shoebox with items for another child his age.

3. Here's a challenge to develop a stewardship mentality in your home: Try NOT to use the words "my, mine, or I" for an entire week in your home among family. If you really want a challenge, try doing it at work but do not tell anyone else at your job.

Chapter 16
The Victim Mentality

It was the most difficult phone call Edna ever had to make. She wondered who else she could call besides her parents but no one came to mind. She sat and stared at the phone for what seemed like an eternity. Dialing the number was surreal until her Dad said, "Hello?" Edna cried out a weak, "Daddy, it's me. I'm so sorry" and that was all she could say as she wept on the phone for a few moments.

Addiction-proof parenting is primarily concerned with helping you and your child to think differently from what this world (and even your flesh) tells you to think. If we are not careful and intentional, we can all slip into a mindset that is detrimental to us, our society, and to the body of Christ. The "addict" develops patterns of thinking that feed the idolatrous desires of the fleshly heart and counteract the work of the Holy Spirit. In the following chapters, we will examine the three remaining mentalities (or mindsets, outlooks, attitudes, patterns of thought), that I see manifested in those I counsel for various addictions.

The final three mentalities are "victim," "perishing," and "rebellious," and each manifests in this particular order based upon Ephesians 5:18-21: **"And do not get drunk with wine, for that is debauchery, but be filled with the Spirit, addressing one another in psalms and hymns and spiritual songs, singing and making melody to the Lord with all your heart, giving thanks always and for everything to God the Father in the name of our Lord Jesus Christ, submitting to one another out of reverence for Christ."**

The self-centered child feeds his little fleshly appetites with whatever the parent allows him to "eat," metaphorically and spiritually-speaking. This feeding frenzy will produce thoughts compatible with the feeding of the flesh. All children are constantly interpreting events and actions around them, and of course, they interpret them in a child-like manner; therefore, if a parent teaches the child that "it is all about you," then of course he will think: "it's all about me!"

Beginning in the child's very first years of life, many parents make excuses for their children's behavior, thereby unwittingly

117

encouraging them to continue in sin and to think like victims. One example is the parent who explains, "Oh, he's just tired" when a four year old child acts rudely when meeting a new adult. Or when a parent excuses bad behavior in a restaurant by saying, "He's just a child." We are raising a nation of "addicts." Children are not helped when they are excused from sin. Children must be held responsible, disciplined in love, and taught to obey their parents beginning at a very young age. Children who do not learn these lessons and are allowed to act irresponsibly and disobediently are more likely to turn to all types of sinful "addictions."

How the Victim Mentality is Fostered

A "victim" mentality is defined in this book as the belief that one has been wronged by another person. This develops into an outlook on life that is self-defeating. They feel powerless though they are not. Sometimes, the offense is real. There are true victims in this world. When a child is wrongly hurt by parents, he may turn to drugs or some other form of idolatry to escape, cope, and deal with the pain. This choice is not God's best for the child and will only lead to further problems.

At other times, a child *perceives* that he has been treated unfairly though he hasn't, and the offense is merely a perception. For various reasons, he believes he should be treated better than he is. Many times the child is tender-hearted so the perceived hurt feels very real and painful. He is interpreting the hurts incorrectly and needs parental love and truth to help him to think, feel, and act biblically. Victims feel powerless because they believe they have been taken advantage of and overpowered.

No matter how the victim mentality develops, it often leads to an addictive outlook toward life. You must not allow your child to develop a victim mentality of feeling like a powerless person who is being taking advantage of by an unfair parent. For example, in Genesis 3:12, Adam blamed his Father God for his sin and the Lord had done nothing to provoke Adam to sin: **"The man said, 'The woman whom you gave to be with me, she gave me fruit of the tree, and I ate.'"** Notice the language here is "the woman whom you gave to be with me" implies some culpability on God's part for Adam's sin. The Lord God had done nothing wrong, yet Adam was blaming God and placing responsibility upon God for Adam's sin.

Every person I know struggles at times with this same tendency to blame God for his/her problems. Many "victims" are angry with God.

God's command to Adam was clear in Genesis 2:17. God spoke with perfect clarity and Adam outright chose to disobey God's Word. Likewise, you must hold your child accountable to clear responsibilities. Communicate your commands and expectations clearly to your children and ask them to repeat what they are hearing from you. Preparatory parenting depends upon good communication by the parent.

For example, I remember attending a social event with my family. In our haste, we hurried to the church social and I was very embarrassed by how my children acted. They would not use basic manners and say "hello" and greet people. My wife and I learned a valuable lesson. At the next church function, we prepared our children in advance by teaching them our expectations for kindly greeting others. At home, we practiced smiling, giving eye contact, saying "Hello, Mrs. Jones," and shaking hands properly. It was a fun time for all of us and a learning time for the children. We reviewed these things again right before the next event and our children responded well. We were so pleased with their good manners and the kindness they showed others at this second event, and we told them so. Preparatory parenting began at home where the expectations were made clear and practiced.

When parents fail to teach their children to take responsibility for their choices by obeying the fifth commandment (**"Honor your father and mother..."**), the result is the victim mentality.[46] The mindset of the addict in active addiction is that he is a victim of his circumstances and yet his life is out of control because he is not doing what is right by God's standards. He is not filled with the Holy Spirit. It is such a defeating mentality that the addict quits trying to battle the addiction and gives up. Though often not a real "victim," he thinks he is and begins acting like one, believing he is "powerless" to overcome the problem.

Blame-shifting is a natural tendency of our flesh when we are

---

[46] This mentality is based upon Ephesians 5:18: **"And do not get drunk with wine, for that is debauchery, but be filled with the Spirit..."** where one is commanded not to act irresponsibly which leads to debauchery, or "utter ruin." When people live this way, they tend to blame others rather than to blame their own choices; thus, the birth of the victim mentality.

confronted with sin. When your child shifts the blame, he believes his sin is the fault of the person he is blaming. In other words, the child thinks the person he is blaming is really "victimizing" him since the sin is this other person's fault. Do not miss this critical point. When a child is allowed to blame others for his sins or mistakes, he will wrongly believe that his poor choices are really someone else's fault.

By allowing your child to believe that his sin is someone else's fault, you complicate matters even more, since he will ultimately blame God for his sin. In that sense, he develops a sinful mindset toward God, who is "victimizing" him, though this is not true at all! Allowing your child to think this way will only lead him away from the love and forgiveness of Jesus Christ, who desires to forgive repentant persons of their sins! Can you begin to see the damage in allowing your children to be irresponsible, disobedient, and blame-shifting for their sinful choices?

What Not to Say

Parents foster the victim mentality in their children at a young age by saying things like this to them:

- "It's Mommy's fault, sweetie, not yours," when it clearly is the child's fault.

- "He didn't mean to say that," when the child clearly meant to say it.

- "I'm sure it was an accident," when the child clearly meant to carry out the behavior.

- To the child directly: "You can't help your thoughts," or "You can't help that you are fearful," when the child can learn to better manage thoughts that lead to feelings. He can learn early in life to think on pure things according to Philippians 4:8.

- "My daughter and son-in-law just fell out of love," when the two of them really began to *think unloving thoughts* about each other leading to actions and feelings that are unloving. Often, unloving thoughts manifest when two people fail to meet each other's unbiblical expectations. Love is a choice to think loving thoughts and to do loving actions toward the person you are choosing to love. No one really ever "falls out of love" as though it were passive. Love is active!

- "Your Daddy didn't mean to say that," which removes responsibility from the parent and sends a clear message to the child that adults do not have to be responsible either.

- "She is just tired," or "She doesn't feel well," to excuse the sinful choice of the child. The child is responsible regardless of his fatigue or illness.

- "He's just shy," which may be true but the child may need to learn not to be rude and to be kind like Christ and say "hello" to someone. Somehow, we've lost our manners in our society!

You can probably think of many more statements like these that excuse responsibility and shift the blame to someone or something else, just as Adam and Eve did in the Garden of Eden in Genesis 3. For addicts specifically, here are some more statements that I hear in biblical counseling sessions:

- "My problems stem from the way I was raised," meaning the person blames his parents and his upbringing for his addictive behavior. (This may be true, but it is an excuse nevertheless.)

- "I gamble just like my Daddy did, so it's a generational curse," meaning the person is just following in the footsteps of a parent because of the curse of sin. Some are blaming Satan. Remember that Adam and Eve were tempted by the serpent and they deliberately chose to disobey God.

- "I was poor so I never had the finer things in life," meaning his environment is to blame.

- "The devil made me do it," or "Satan is causing me to sin," is blaming Satan, which is a half-truth, but the problem is most likely caused by a sinful choice.

- "I can't stop shopping," when the person really means "I won't stop shopping and spending money irresponsibly."

- "When people make me angry, I cut myself and self-injure," when the person has not learned how to do what is right when other people provoke them to anger. Living by feelings is common with addicts, but they must learn to do what is right no matter how they feel. They must say "no" to the flesh and "yes" to the Holy Spirit (Ephesians 5:18).

- "I need to be delivered from my fear and anger." One is never "delivered" from emotions like fear and anger because they are necessary to live. Proper fear helps to protect someone and proper anger helps to resolve problems. Fear and anger are emotions necessary to live.

- "I need God to deliver me from my desire for sex," or "I need God to deliver me from my desire to work excessively." Sex, work, sleep, food, and drink are physical appetites that God placed in us for a good reason; therefore, like emotions, He will not "deliver" us from these natural appetites. Instead, He will help us to learn to be more balanced in our fulfillment of all of these appetites. A normal desire for these appetites is healthy, not too much or too little, and these appetites must be satisfied in a non-sinful manner.

- "I just lose track of time when I play that internet game," which is true, but we are still responsible to set boundaries and limits upon the time spent playing a video game so we fulfill all our responsibilities.

- "Who are you to tell me to get sober?" is a manipulative twist that gets the attention off the addict and onto a flawed parent. The standard is not the parent but is Christ and His Word.

- "I've tried to pray and read my Bible, but God just isn't showing up to help me with my sexual sin."

- "It's not my fault."

- "I cannot do anything about it because it's not my fault." There is a deep sense of hopelessness in this statement. That is why the "victim mentality" is so devastating—it leads to hopelessness.

Again, there are an infinite number of examples like the above and all of them have blame-shifting involved in some measure. Blame-shifting is the oldest excuse in the Bible and children do not have to learn to be effective at shifting the blame. Blame-shifting comes quite naturally to all of us, especially young children.

I encourage you to think of your own statements that shift the blame and promote a victim mentality. Think about some things that both you and your child have said that have deflected responsibility and shifted the blame to someone or something else. Ask a trusted Christian friend to help you if you cannot think of anything specific.

Sometimes another person has to help us to see where we have "blind spots."

Sin is Personal with the Lord

David wrote Psalm 51:4, which states: **"Against you, you only, have I sinned and done what is evil in your sight, so that you may be justified in your words and blameless in your judgment."** David knew his sin of adultery and conspiracy to murder was ultimately against the Lord, though he had sinned against people. That is not to suggest that David did not have to repent to those persons and to ask them for forgiveness.

Your child's choices to sin are not personal attacks against you. Too many parents are offended, shocked, and angered when their children sinfully disobey them. You are the authority figure God has placed over your children. Their sin is the by-product of their lack of trust in God and the rebellion of their flesh. Sin always involves an evil, unbelieving, and distrustful heart toward God according to Hebrews 3:12: **"Take care, brothers, lest there be in any of you an evil, unbelieving heart, leading you to fall away from the living God."**

Furthermore, when you remove the responsibility of your child's wrong choices you miss the opportunity to lead them to the grace of God, who is willing to forgive them from all of their unrighteousness through Christ Jesus. The following examples are parental statements that remove responsibility from the child and promote the victim mentality:

- "It's not your fault that you struck out. That ball was way outside. The umpire was blind."
- "I know you didn't mean to do that, Honey."
- "I don't have any respect for that teacher. She is not a good teacher at all."
- "You're just tired. You need a nap."
- "You're sick right now. That's why you are acting so badly."
- "I'm sure that was just a mistake" (when it really was a sinful choice with purpose).
- "He's not used to playing with girls, so he is a little rough."

- "She's on drugs because her mother was on drugs."
- "Addiction just runs in the family. There's no avoiding it."
- "He was always a happy young man until she broke up with him. Then, he turned to drugs because she broke his heart."
- "It's just part of his disease of addiction."
- "You cannot do anything about it because it's not your fault."

I see many parents with young children who can't understand why their children cannot sit still in church, school, or a Sunday school class. These parents will slap their child and in an angry tone say, "You know we are in church, so why don't you sit still?" These parents are constantly disappointed in their children when they disobey because their expectation of perfection is unrealistic. Your child will sin and make bad choices. Plan on it. But do some preparatory parenting for the church service at home where you can freely administer the rod and reproof.

Expect imperfection and wrong choices so that you will not be devastated when it happens. Those choices are a product of hearts that are bent toward doing things to please themselves. As a parent who understands their sinful natures, I am not shocked or even surprised when my children make a sinful choice. I do not permit it or alleviate the consequence for the wrong choice, but I am not surprised by it. I plan to discipline in accordance with God's Word. I hold the child responsible to God's standards and not to legalistic standards set by human parents that may be unrealistic, legalistic, and perfectionistic.

Few things will provoke children to anger like perfectionism. Do not be a parent who falls for that lie of Satan. Make your standards God's standards found in His Word. Hold your child responsible but do not expect perfection. The problem with perfectionism is that it ignores grace, and we are created in *dire need* of God's grace. Be balanced in these two areas of your parenting and you will be doing addiction-proof parenting.

Conclusion

Scripture teaches that God is sovereign, but man is also responsible. God is one hundred percent sovereign and mankind is one hundred percent responsible for his choices. Both of these concepts are true and taught simultaneously in the Bible. This truth is not illogical but is supra-logical, meaning that only God is capable of understanding it fully.

In light of these biblical truths, teach your child that God is sovereign and allows mankind to make sinful choices. However, God is redemptive and He is capable of turning our sins into a blessing for us. For example, in Genesis 37, Joseph's brothers sold him into slavery, which was sinful. However, God used that very wrong choice to save Joseph's brothers' lives as Joseph rose to power (Genesis 41:37-56), which resulted in providing food and a new land for them (Genesis 45:21-24 & Genesis 47). Only God can turn our worst, sinful choices into something that ends up saving our lives. God saves us from our sins and, though not always, sometimes from the consequences of our sins.

KEY IDEAS AND PRACTICAL THINGS TO DO

1. Read and write out Ephesians 5:18-21 to discuss with your older children at a family devotion.

2. List your God-given responsibilities and evaluate on a scale from 1 to 10 how well you are fulfilling them.

3. Evaluate your language in terms of the words you use that encourage the victim mentality. Take one week and write down each time you use victim terminology. Next to each word or phrase, replace them with a biblical alternative that is truthful and acceptable. If needed, ask a trusted Christian friend for help.

Chapter 17
Too Much Responsibility

Needless to say, Edna's parents were devastated as they sat in the juvenile detention center. "We thought we raised you better than this, Edna" was the last thing Edna heard them say as she was escorted to her juvenile cell. Edna's parents decided to allow her to experience the consequences from her poor choices and Edna never tried alcohol or drugs again in her life.

When parents blur the lines of responsibility in a child's mind, they create confusion, causing the child to wonder, "What is expected of me?" Unclear responsibilities provoke the child to frustration leading to a victim mentality, or the perception that he has been victimized, wronged, and taken advantage of.

Children may incorrectly learn responsibility in two extremes, which affect their productivity later as adults. First, they are not taught to take enough responsibility. As adults they have either not learned what God and society requires of them or they have learned to blame others for their failures. Second, some children are forced to take on too much responsibility that should not belong to them and they feel overwhelmed and burdened by it. They do not learn what God requires of them biblically or they wrongly believe they are obligated to more responsibilities than are necessary. Both extremes have damaging effects.

Unfortunately it is all too common, especially in single parent households; to see that a child has been given so much responsibility that he or she begins to take on the role of parent. This is not healthy for anyone in the family. The importance of this mentality cannot be over-emphasized as you will see when we apply it to the sin of drunkenness. (Note: the Bible does not call it alcoholism.)

The issue of taking responsibility and being obedient to the Holy Spirit is mentioned first in the passage that addresses drunkenness and "addiction" in Ephesians 5:18-21 (v.18 only): **"And do not get drunk with wine, for that is debauchery, but be filled with the Spirit..."** There is no way around it: a Spirit-filled life is one in which a person makes righteous decisions that please the Lord. Being responsible and obedient to the Holy Spirit is the very first command to counter drunkenness. A drunkard is irresponsible. A drunkard is disobedient to God. A drunkard is not under the power of the Holy Spirit but under the power of his own flesh. Therefore, the drunkard is filled with his flesh and not the Spirit, whereby he fulfills the desires of his flesh and not the desires of God.

From this verse in Ephesians 5:18, it is derived that the antidote for drunkenness is the filling of the Holy Spirit, which always leads to right choices of responsibility and obedience to Christ. This is the first requirement that God places upon any transforming addict from any type of addiction: responsibility—rather than being drunk with wine and out of control.

Most drunkards are living in one of two extremes: too little or too much responsibility. Both of these extremes contribute to a victim mentality. Those who are taking too little responsibility have free time to devote to an "addiction" and those who are taking too much responsibility have an excuse of feeling overwhelmed and desiring an "escape" to turn to an "addiction."

Too Much Responsibility

Do not parent to the extreme that makes a child responsible for things that are not his or her responsibility. For example, parents unwittingly provoke their children to be anxious when they say things like, "You need to study for your test so that you can make a 100% tomorrow." This type of statement places responsibility upon the child for an outcome that may be beyond his or her control. Instead, a biblically-minded parent says: "Study as hard as you can tonight so that you will do your best tomorrow. Pray that the Lord will help you to do your best." Effort is emphasized in this last statement. As a parent, you want to emphasize effort over ability since children are always responsible for the effort they put forth, though their abilities may be limited.

Children have different abilities. I have four children and all four have unique gifts and talents. I do not expect them to be perfect in all areas. Ability is different from effort. I do expect them to put forth their best efforts at chores, homework, reading the Bible, and other tasks that are their responsibilities to fulfill. However, based upon their abilities, I know that some of my children excel at certain tasks while others struggle at those same tasks. Therefore, I do not evaluate them based upon ability but upon effort. "Did you do your best?" is a question I ask often. If they say "yes," I praise them (unless I know better!).

Being Too Child-centered and not Christ-centered

When a home is child-centered rather than Christ-centered, the child may develop a victim mentality because he has been deceived into thinking he is the "king" of the home. He then becomes frustrated when the parents take back the authority that rightfully belongs to them in the first place. The parents are "creating a monster" in the child in terms of his attitude.

For example, a mother asks her preschool-aged child, "What do you want to eat for lunch today?" even though the mother has planned to have spaghetti. The child answers, "I want potato chips and a cookie, Mommy." A diet of chips and cookies is not healthy and the parent wants what is best for the child; however, by appearing to give the child a choice, Mommy has created a problem that will lead to frustration for both! Mommy now has to say, "I've made spaghetti for us. Maybe after you eat it, you can have chips and a cookie." The child likely responds angrily, "No, Mommy, I don't want spaghetti," and screams and cries loudly. Mommy's mistake was to give a choice to a child who was not in a position to make a wise decision. The choice was not real for the child and, as a result, brought a sense of powerlessness which sows a seed of the victim mentality in the child. Also, the mother has simply provoked her child to anger with a mindless question that turned into a larger issue.

As a parent, you must limit your child's choices. In fact, I recommend giving him little or no choices for the first few developmental years for the purpose of teaching him to obey your commands. We learned this parenting lesson when our children were very young: Imagine a funnel that is turned upside down. Keep the "funnel of responsibility" narrow in the beginning and widen the funnel as he proves himself responsible enough to make godly choices. Limiting choices is good for children and parents alike.

Eliminate questions that ask your child, "would you like...?" or "what do you want...?" or "where do you want to go?" He does not need to make those decisions. Instead, children need to obey the parent who makes those decisions. They must learn to take commands from parents in the early years and to be obedient and responsible to those commands. Your home is not a democracy that gives your child an equal vote!

Please understand that the limitation of choices is *not* a limitation of responsibilities! Be sure to hold your children responsible for tasks that they can accomplish, but do not give them a *choice* as to whether or not they want to *do* the task or not. Enforce the call to obedience with your children by following up to be sure they do the task required. Place responsibilities on the children that are age-appropriate, meaning you do not expect a two-year old to take out the trash!

My wife often tells a personal story that relates to this area of parenting. When our first child was barely three years old, she read somewhere in a parenting magazine that to increase our child's self-esteem, we need to give him as many choices in life as possible—that we, as his parents, should be looking for areas in which he can have control so as to not exasperate him. This is the exact opposite of what the Bible says, but we had not learned this principle yet. So my wife began to allow our precious three year old to choose what he wanted to wear each day that summer.

Each day they would open up the chest of drawers together and have the same conversation: "What do you want to wear today, sweetie?" "The Lakers shirt, Mommy," he would say each day. "Okay, honey, that's fine." This went on for days, and even weeks, until my wife decided that the only viable option was to give away the Lakers shirt. She felt she couldn't tell him no; after all, it was easy to toss the Lakers shirt into the wash with the baby's wash each day (we had an 18 month old at the same time), so it wasn't that much of an inconvenience to her. And sometimes she just let him wear it dirty a couple of days in a row: "What harm is there in that?" she would think. She thought that it would hurt his feelings and damage his self-esteem if she told him she didn't want him to wear the Lakers shirt again, but at the same time she knew it was not best for him to wear the same shirt every day of his life! She just didn't know *why* it wasn't good for him. It was just a Lakers jersey!

Much heartache and tears (her's and our son's) followed those days as she tried to figure out where she went wrong. After all, she did what the parenting magazine said to do. Three years later we were taught the funnel analogy of parenting and what God has to say about parenting in the Bible. What refreshing teaching at such a crucial time in our parenting lives!

If you give a child too many choices, encouraging him to take responsibilities that are not his, then you are also giving him too much power to make decisions that are not his to make. It will provoke the child to frustration when you *attempt to reclaim the power* you gave him. This is one way we fail to obey God when he tells us that we are not to provoke our children to anger (Ephesians 6:4). Your child will become angry. Though not a true victim, he will feel victimized by the conflicting messages sent to him in this type of situation.

There are true victims in life. A true victim is someone who has been adversely affected by someone else's sin without having provoked him or contributed to the problem. When someone steals from your car, you are victimized by someone's sinful action. Victimization occurs when someone violates one of the Ten Commandments or one of society's laws which are designed to protect people and demonstrate respect and love to others.

However, many who are ensnared to all types of "addiction" wrongly believe they are being treated harshly and unfairly, and that they are victims when in reality they are not. It is their perception that is warped. As a parent, do not encourage this devastating mindset by giving your child too much power and responsibility in life. Allow your child to be in the proper role of a child in your home.

The Consequences of Taking on Too Much Responsibility

Some children are elevated to a position of power and influence in the family that is not their role. These children embrace the opportunity to be "adult-like" and sometimes end up being more parental than the parent. This is most evident in homes ravaged by alcohol and drugs. When parents turn to alcohol and drugs, their children, who are not spiritually or physically ready to enter this adult world, often have no choice but to do so. Then, when they do become adults, they mistakenly believe they must continue to take care of their irresponsible, drug-using parents. It is very confusing to the child, even when they become adults, to biblically sort out their responsibilities.

For example, a son whose mother chose to be a drunkard for most of his life may grow up continuing to think: "I've got to help my mom." Even after he is married, he will call his mom frequently to check on her. He tells his mom things that he forgets to tell his wife. Thus, the "leave and cleave" principle of marriage in Genesis 2:24 is being habitually ignored. His wife feels threatened and fearful when he gives his mother money or a place to stay often beyond his own means to do so. The mother may at times play on his sympathies and deceive him to manipulate him for financial help. The son believes he is caught between his wife and his mother, yet he can't let go of feeling he is responsible for the care of his mother. Before long the son believes he is the victim in this emotional triangle and that he has lost control of his life. He turns to alcohol as an escape, thinking it will help him deal with the stress.

All of this behavior is complicated and packed with emotion and it started with wrong interpretations from childhood about biblical responsibilities. This is an issue that the secular world calls being an "adult child of an addict" because the home is reversing the responsibilities of the parents and the children, which results in confusion.

The Lord wants you to possess and apply His wisdom for your family. He wants you to build your spiritual home according to His blueprints which are found in His Word of truth. God has created roles for your family to fulfill to bring peace, harmony, and love into your home.

KEY IDEAS AND PRACTICAL THINGS TO DO

1. List your God-given responsibilities as a parent and ask a trusted Christian friend to help you to determine if these responsibilities belong to you or not. Put a line through each one that God does not want you to take.

2. List excessive responsibilities that you have placed upon your child, which must be replaced or deleted. Evaluate the words and phrases you use that emphasize taking on too much responsibility as well.

3. Read the *Gospel Primer* by Milton Vincent with your child to remind yourselves of the powerful message of the Gospel.

Chapter 18
Too Little Responsibility

Freddie's parents were called in the middle of the night to return home from their lake house. Freddie confessed everything to his parents who were disappointed in their son's poor choices; however, because they had a relationship with Christ, Freddie's parents understood forgiveness. Freddie's parents held him responsible for his sinful choices and provided for him to meet with a biblical counselor. Through this process of biblical counseling, Freddie experienced the forgiveness of Christ personally, made a profession of faith in Christ, and surrendered his life to be lived for the glory of God.

Because we are human beings created in His image for His own glory, God holds all of us responsible for our thoughts, words, and actions. Only a person who has a physical problem stemming from legitimate organic causes that prohibit him from thinking, speaking, or acting appropriately is held less responsible for his choices. However, the world's system is often too quick to excuse a person's bad behavior by blaming their environment or a so-called disease. Addiction is now predominantly viewed as an illness and a disease rather than a sin nature problem that becomes physically enslaving. However, before God, the "addict" is held responsible for his or her thoughts and actions that *led to* the "addiction."

What are a person's God-given responsibilities? There are two kinds of responsibilities: those given to all mankind and those that are specific for certain roles. Responsibilities given to all mankind include obeying the Ten Commandments and other directives in Scripture that God expects all persons to honor and fulfill. For example, "Thou shall not steal" is a command to all persons regardless of age, gender, or other differences. Responsibilities given to specific people include the command for husbands to love their wives as Christ loved the church (Ephesians 5:25), for children to obey their parents in the Lord (Ephesians 6:1), and for servants (i.e. workers/ employees today) to be submissive to their masters (i.e. employers in today's culture) according to 1 Peter 2:18. God expects us to read His Word and to obey His commands because it glorifies Him and is in our best interests, since He alone knows what is best for His children. We are to trust Him. Obeying His commands is one way to be responsible and to trust God.

Some parents accept too much of their child's responsibilities before God, thereby placing too little responsibility upon their children—which is commonly called "enabling." For the adult child this may include doing their work, paying their bills, planning and finishing their projects. For the young child, it may mean excusing them from contributing to the smooth functioning of the household. These parents take on more of the responsibility, and later, they blame themselves for their child's poor performance and productivity. Like Cain in Genesis 4, the child knows he is failing to live up to God's requirements, which produces anger and depression.

This tendency to "enable" feeds a victim mentality. The child is held responsible by God. His parents are not doing their child any favors by taking on those responsibilities since it is the child who will experience the consequences of failing to obey God.

Some of the God-given responsibilities placed upon your child pertain to his thoughts, words, and deeds. For example, a child who is obsessively thinking about video games will predominantly talk about those games and may throw a temper tantrum when he is denied opportunities to play them. God holds that child accountable for all of his thoughts, words, and actions surrounding the desire to play video games. It is idolatry at the lowest level. Do not allow your child to throw a temper tantrum without some form of loving, instructive discipline with consequences because that child is disobeying God.

Obviously, you do not want to see your child fail or be hurt, but worse than that is a parent's "enabling" reaction. As parents, you must sometimes allow your children to fail. It is not your job to rescue them every time they fail. When a child is not held responsible for his thoughts, words, and actions, his parents are "enabling" him to sin.

For example, a child in fifth grade skips school and is caught. When disciplined by the school with a suspension, the mother is ashamed and inconvenienced. Instead of accepting it and using it for a teaching time, the mother complains to the principal and publicly causes a scene. In her sinful behavior, the mother persuasively leads the principal to relent and the child is not suspended. In her pride, the mother thinks she has "successfully" rescued her child from the painful consequence of being suspended from school and the embarrassment to his "self-image" and hers. The mother's pattern is to always rescue her child from any perceived, "hurtful" consequences. But what message is really being sent to the child? That it is okay to break rules because mother will bail you out of the consequences.

Fast forward in time, that same child grows up, goes to college, and the poor choices continue but with greater consequences. Now, the child is choosing to smoke marijuana with the "wrong friends" and driving under the influence of mind-altering drugs. There is no "fear of God"[47] in the child or even fear of getting caught by the police because he has always been rescued from the consequences of his sinful choices. It is only a matter of time before the child will face consequences from which there is no escape.

Instead of "enabling" your child, call him to repentance to Christ so that he may be reconciled with Him. Hold him responsible before the Lord, not just to you as a parent. Help your child to set his mind on the things of God and not just the things of man (Matthew 16:23).

Controlling

When parents take on too much responsibility, they are perceived as "controlling" by the child. "You are a control freak, Mom," is what a teen-ager might say when his parent is taking on responsibilities that belong to him. I hate to burst your parental bubble, but when a parent takes on the child's responsibilities and "enables" him to live irresponsibly, the consequences are devastating. Often, it is a parent's love of control that feeds this behavior of "enabling" the child to sin and be irresponsible. At the core, this parent is not trusting God.

A parent who loves control and takes on too much responsibility makes statements like:

"I want it done this way and no other way."

"I can do this better than anyone else."

"No one else will do this if I don't do it."

"It's all my fault," parents will say when the responsibility really lies on the child's shoulders!

A parent who is too controlling will think that he is the only one who knows what is best for the child and that he must be the one to save and change him. The controlling parent is often riddled with

---

[47] Psalms 14:1.

fear, anger, guilt, and has a problem trusting God.[48] Sinful fear is often in the heart of the controlling parent who thinks he knows better than the Lord.

Quite often, children will take responsibility for only the bare minimum of what is expected of them. God has called us to be productive, obedient Christians in the areas of our financial, social, physical, religious, and personal lives, but those in addiction are not fulfilling these responsibilities. They expect God or others to do their job. When this happens, children feel like a victim and think they are powerless to control their circumstances. Later in life, an enabling spouse or parent may be involved in taking on many of their responsibilities.

For a practical example, let's say that a mother in active addiction is failing to raise her children. She drops them off at the grandparents' house frequently. The grandparents end up raising her children while she becomes less of a parental influence. Though God has given the responsibility and authority to the parent, she has abdicated that role by giving it to the grandparents who accept the role because of their love for their grandchildren. It is a very confusing situation for all persons involved. In time, the parent who has shirked her responsibility may develop bitterness toward her parents (the grandparents) though their heart is to merely be a help to her.

The Cycle of the Victim Mentality

The resulting mindset of this cycle has even more damaging consequences. As the child takes less responsibility and a parent takes more of those responsibilities, the child develops an angry and depressed attitude. Why? The answer is that he knows he is failing in this area but is not willing to change. This internal conflict breeds his anger toward his parents.

When someone sins by omission, or by failing to do what is rightly required by the Lord, there are consequences for those sins because mankind is under the curse of the sin resulting from the fall of Adam and Eve in Genesis 3. Just as we are under the law of gravity, we are also under the law of sin and its consequences, which

---

[48] Parents can read my book, *Divine Intervention*, to learn more about how to deal with family members who are "idolaters" and "addicts."

always result in separation from God, sinful emotional responses, and eternal death. When Adam and Eve sinned in Genesis 3, the emotions of fear and shame appeared for the first time in human history. The sinful failures of a person in addiction to be responsible are compounded by their wrong thinking—the victim mentality. Here is a typical cycle:

- an addict fails to be responsible,
- a parent picks up the responsibility for the addict,
- the addict feels guilty about the sinful failure,
- the sin causes consequential emotions (depression),
- the addict mistakenly begins to believe that he is not responsible and that the parent is responsible, and finally,
- the addict becomes angry at the parent, sometimes unknowingly.

It is incredible to see how many addicts are bitter and hateful toward their parents who are simply trying to do the right thing by filling the void left by the addict's irresponsibility. Parents are often shocked at the angry attitude of a child whom they are "enabling" to be irresponsible. The parent thinks, "I am only trying to help my child—why doesn't he see it?" While it may look like victimization to the child who desires to be in control of his own life, the parent does not see it. The parent simply believes he is doing the right thing by taking care of the responsibilities, but the consequences of the sin are designed by the Lord to point the person back to Christ for confession, repentance, forgiveness, and power to do the will of God. The dynamics of a "rescuing" or "enabling" parent who takes the responsibility from a child is acting sinfully, which will provoke that child to anger.

Though the child may not be able to verbalize it, he knows that he is failing to be responsible to his God-given responsibilities. For a high school student this may include failing to complete school projects, not maintaining and communicating his calendar of events with his parents, and not submitting to the order of the house rules. By God's design, all sin produces consequences including emotions like guilt, anger, and depression. These consequences manifest in order to lead a sinning person to confession and repentance. Even though the parents mistakenly believe they are helping the child, they are actually sinning and contributing to the child's sinful failures to be responsible. Unfortunately, it is a double whammy of sin: the child's and the parent's!

Cain's Wrong Response

To better illustrate this point, read this lengthy passage in Genesis 4:1-16 about Cain's sin and relationship to the Lord:

> Now Adam knew Eve his wife, and she conceived and bore Cain, saying, "I have gotten a man with the help of the Lord." And again, she bore his brother Abel. Now Abel was a keeper of sheep, and Cain a worker of the ground. In the course of time Cain brought to the Lord an offering of the fruit of the ground, and Abel also brought of the firstborn of his flock and of their fat portions. And the Lord had regard for Abel and his offering, but for Cain and his offering he had no regard. So Cain was very angry, and his face fell. The Lord said to Cain, "Why are you angry, and why has your face fallen? If you do well, will you not be accepted? And if you do not do well, sin is crouching at the door. Its desire is for you, but you must rule over it."
>
> Cain spoke to Abel his brother. And when they were in the field, Cain rose up against his brother Abel and killed him. Then the Lord said to Cain, "Where is Abel your brother?" He said, "I do not know; am I my brother's keeper?" And the Lord said, "What have you done? The voice of your brother's blood is crying to me from the ground. And now you are cursed from the ground, which has opened its mouth to receive your brother's blood from your hand. When you work the ground, it shall no longer yield to you its strength. You shall be a fugitive and a wanderer on the earth." Cain said to the Lord, "My punishment is greater than I can bear. Behold, you have driven me today away from the ground, and from your face I shall be hidden. I shall be a fugitive and a wanderer on the earth, and whoever finds me

will kill me." Then the LORD said to him, "Not so! If anyone kills Cain, vengeance shall be taken on him sevenfold." And the LORD put a mark on Cain, lest any who found him should attack him. Then Cain went away from the presence of the LORD and settled in the land of Nod, east of Eden."

Because of the seriousness of sin and disobedience, recall that God made **"garments of skins and clothed"** Adam and Eve (Genesis 3:21), which meant that God required the blood sacrifice of animals in order to provide clothing for them. The righteous justice of God also required perfectly righteous blood to be shed at Calvary, and Jesus' blood that was shed on the cross for the atonement of sin fully satisfied the perfect wrath of God (John 19:34; 1 Peter 1:19). Many times the sacrifice was a perfect lamb. Jesus was the perfect Lamb of God (John 1:29).

In verse 5 above, Cain's sacrifice was substandard according to God's requirement of a blood sacrifice. To make matters worse, Cain responded sinfully to his own act of disobedience to God's standard by becoming angry and depressed ("face fallen"). Cain's actions and poor sacrifice were not pleasing to God, which produced emotions in Cain that were designed to lead him to repentance, but he did not repent and even sinned further. Therefore, we see God "parent" and "counsel" Cain by asking him four questions in verses 6, 7, 9, and 10. Although God knew the answer to all of these questions, it appeared that Cain was not aware of it. Like any good parent or counselor, God's questions were designed to cause Cain to be reflective and to analyze his heart motives behind his sinful choices and the resulting emotions. Sadly, Cain never took responsibility for his wrong-doing. He never confessed his sin and he failed to cry out to God to forgive him. In verse 16, Cain walked away from a relationship with the Lord rather than walking with God.

As a good Parent, God held Cain responsible in verse 7 with a parental warning: **"And if you do not do well, sin is crouching at the door. Its desire is for you, but you must rule over it."** Cain was responsible to rule over sin, which was depicted as a wild beast that desired to overtake and devour Cain if he let it. Unfortunately, Cain allowed sin to overtake him in the next verse when he purposely murdered his brother, Abel. When God again asked Cain a gracious question calling him to be honest and take responsibility for his sin,

Cain added dishonesty (v. 9) to his anger and depression and then gave a sarcastic response to God the Father in verses 13-14: **"Cain said to the LORD, 'My punishment is greater than I can bear. Behold, you have driven me today away from the ground, and from your face I shall be hidden. I shall be a fugitive and a wanderer on the earth, and whoever finds me will kill me.'"** There was still a hint of blaming God in Cain's statement even for the righteous decision the Lord made.

After his just consequence was pronounced by the Lord, Cain was still unrepentant, claiming that his punishment was too great in verse 13. In His mercy, God protected Cain from harm and Cain still rejected the grace of God designed to bring him to repentance. God never took away Cain's responsibility to battle and overcome sin. God intervened but Cain was responsible for his own choices though he never acknowledged it according to this passage of Scripture.

Because God's grace was ready and waiting for Cain's repentance, all Cain had to do was take responsibility for his sinful choices at any point along the way, but he refused to do so. Cain shifted the blame for his substandard sacrifice and his resulting anger and depression onto his brother, Abel. In many ways, Cain acted like a victim of his circumstances and emotions though he was precisely to blame for them! God never let Cain be a victim in their conversations and simply asked questions of Cain so that he could confess his sins and receive the wonderful forgiveness God offers all sinners in Jesus Christ.

A mother who was using drugs and living with a drug dealer temporarily lost her child to the Department of Human Resources. The child went to foster care and was shuffled from home to home for several months. When the mother got her act together and stopped seeing the drug dealer, she was given custody of her child who returned to her home. Understandably, the ten year-old child was angry at her mother and God for the episode of her life where she lived with strangers. Her mother wrongly gave the little girl the following horrible explanation: "We don't know why God did this. All we know is that He has a reason."

This statement only provoked the child to anger. It misrepresented God and the truth. The truth was that the mother had made selfish, sinful choices. These choices caused the government to step in to protect the child from her mother's wrong choices that endangered the child. If the mother were truly repentant, she should have said:

"God allowed this to happen because of my sin. God was protecting you from Mommy's bad choices. Will you forgive me just as Christ has forgiven me?"

God lovingly protected the child from harm utilizing the governmental authorities, but the mother painted a picture of God as the Person to blame for the upheaval. God allowed the mother to make the sinful choices just as He allowed Cain to make his sinful choices. God did not cause the sin and consequences in the child's life, but that was the message sent to the little girl, who is still angry at God and her mother to this day. The little girl despises church and is fearful to go into church services because she has a wrong view of God. She is a true victim. Her addicted mother is not a true victim but acts like one, having propagated sinful thinking in both of their minds. The cyclical dynamics of the victim mentality have devastating consequences.

Blame-Shifting: Too Little Responsibility

What is the oldest trick in the Book (the Bible) when one is taking too little responsibility? The answer is blame-shifting, especially when we are guilty of sin! Genesis 3:8-13 gives us the biblical account of the first act of disobedience against our loving God. Mankind's subsequent response of shifting the blame to someone or something else is clear right from the first book of the Bible:

> **And they heard the sound of the LORD God walking in the garden in the cool of the day, and the man and his wife hid themselves from the presence of the LORD God among the trees of the garden. But the LORD God called to the man and said to him, "Where are you?" And he said, "I heard the sound of you in the garden, and I was afraid, because I was naked, and I hid myself." He said, "Who told you that you were naked? Have you eaten of the tree of which I commanded you not to eat?" The man said, "The woman whom you gave to be with me, she gave me fruit of the tree, and I ate." Then the LORD God said to the woman, "What is this that you have done?" The woman said, "The serpent deceived me, and I ate."**

Adam and Eve were hiding from the presence of the Lord and even tried to make fig leaf garments to cover their sin from God. How sad! They knew they were wrong because they attempted to hide it in these two ways: 1) dressing in fig leaves and 2) hiding in the trees. Your child may also try to hide the truth from you even when the evidence is literally all over the child's face, like cookie crumbs from the cookie jar. You almost want to laugh when the child says, "No, Mommy, I didn't eat any cookies," as they wipe the crumbs from their face. That is the way Adam and Eve looked to God when they were caught hiding in the trees dressed in fig leaves!

Obviously, children come pre-wired with blame-shifting ability because they are born with a sinful nature (Genesis 5:3; Ephesians 4:17-22; Colossians 3:7-11), but parents often reinforce blame-shifting in their children at very young ages. Parents say things like, "I know you didn't mean to slap your sister," thinking that the child needs to hear this for the purpose of not damaging her "self-esteem."[49] A statement like that massages the parent's conscience while they are denying the reality of sin in the child.

No parent wants to think their child is a selfish, self-centered, little sinner. It's horrible to think about the reality of unrepentant sin in your child which leads to problems in this life and ultimately to hell in the next life. Therefore, many parents suppress and deny this truth (Romans 1:18), and that denial will prevent the parent from sharing the "good news" which is the Gospel—that God forgives repentant sinners (responsible for their own sin) who call upon Jesus Christ for forgiveness. Your child needs the Gospel to point him to his sin, and ultimately to his Savior.

Teaching your child to take responsibility when he is blame-shifting is the first essential component of addiction-proof parenting. Rarely does an "addict" take full responsibility for his or her actions. Why? The answer is that he chooses to deny the reality of his sin in order to continue to use the drug or activity of his choice. Romans 1:18-25 plainly states the progression of what a lack of responsibility

---

[49] The parent values "self-esteem" too highly and does not want to see the sin in the child. None of us want to believe that our precious baby is selfish with wicked desires in the heart, but that is precisely why Christ died so violently upon the Cross for all of us. I prefer the term "Christ-esteem" rather than "self-esteem" since our self-worth is found only in Christ.

(which is denying the truth of God's Word) leads to—a darkened mind and a life characterized by sin:

> For the wrath of God is revealed from heaven against all ungodliness and unrighteousness of men, who by their unrighteousness suppress the truth. For what can be known about God is plain to them, because God has shown it to them. For his invisible attributes, namely, his eternal power and divine nature, have been clearly perceived, ever since the creation of the world, in the things that have been made. So they are without excuse. For although they knew God, they did not honor him as God or give thanks to him, but they became futile in their thinking, and their foolish hearts were darkened. Claiming to be wise, they became fools, and exchanged the glory of the immortal God for images resembling mortal man and birds and animals and reptiles. Therefore God gave them up in the lusts of their hearts to impurity, to the dishonoring of their bodies among themselves, because they exchanged the truth about God for a lie and worshiped and served the creature rather than the Creator, who is blessed forever! Amen.

People who remain in bondage to sexual sins, using drugs, or any other "addiction," are blaming others for their choices and exchanging the truth about God for a lie. They *prefer* to believe lies so that they can continue to worship themselves and feed the desires of their flesh. They choose to sin. They are creatures who want to be their own god so they can do whatever they want—even if it destroys them. The reality is that they are not the Creator and one day they will be required to give an account to God for their actions, words, and thoughts.

As a parent, the reality that your child wants to be his own master must motivate you on a daily basis. Is your child sitting on the "throne" in your home, meaning that he is acting like the king and ruler of your home? Does your home center around your children and their schedule, their food choices, nap times, and their happiness? A child-centered home contributes to their anger and frustration because at some level they know that they hold the wrong place in the home. A child is to be a submissive, responsible understudy to the parents who have full authority in the home. Do not encourage a life of leisure and pleasure over and above a life of being responsible and faithful. Allow your children to have fun by being children while teaching them the responsibilities of life in the process.

Dealing With Sin

Some parents "enable" their child to continue to sin in the name of "grace." This is fundamentally wrong! The Bible never endorses the notion that a person should "enable" another person to sin. Even worse, the Bible never endorses that type of thinking and acting as "grace." God does not give grace to us so we may continue to sin. God's perfect purpose for the grace He gives is so that we will cry out to Him, and confess the wrongs we have committed so that He may bestow His great love on us and redeem us from a life filled with sin.

Ultimately, as a parent, you want to encourage your child and you should. However, you must not allow him to shift the blame for his poor choices onto someone or something else. Even when someone sins against him, he is required by God in Romans 12:21: **"Do not be overcome by evil, but overcome evil with good."** There is never an excuse to sin and sin is never a mistake. Apart from organically-caused factors such as a legitimate physical illness, God holds man responsible for all thinking and acting according to His moral standard.

Teach your child that God forgives us when we confess and take responsibility for our sins and trust in Jesus Christ alone to atone for our sins. What happens to an unrepentant, unwilling, and unbelieving person according to the Bible? God says that person will spend an eternity in hell as punishment for those sins. When we take responsibility for our sins before a holy God, we will find His mercy abundantly present to forgive us of our sins based upon Christ alone.

Do not say things that remove responsibility from your child, such as, "Oh, she is just tired and stressed out today. That's why she was disrespectful to me. She's having a bad day." When you do, you are giving them an excuse to sin when they are feeling stressed out. It is never okay to sin. Instead, encourage your child to be responsible and to take responsibility for sinful failures, in spite of challenging circumstances such as a lack of sleep or an especially stressful day.

Children don't need to be taught how to make excuses. A teacher of a learning-challenged student scolded his student for not completing his assignment. The young man responded, "Well, what would you expect from a handicapped kid?" We may smile, but he had already excused himself from even basic responsibility. The teacher appropriately responded, "You may be handicapped, but you can still be trustworthy and responsible."

Label and identify the sin for your child. Use biblical words to do so. For example, do not allow your adult child, who chooses to drink excessively, to call her problem a "disease" or "illness," when the Bible clearly describes this sin as "drunkenness" and "idolatry." We must not ever re-label or excuse sin. When we call sin another name, we are offending a holy God and promoting the victim mentality in the sinner. Sinners need to confess their sins and ask God to forgive them. If we never call drunkenness by its proper biblical name, and instead re-label it as a disease or an illness, then we will never see it as sin and come to a place where we can receive the forgiveness of Christ. Who needs Christ's forgiveness if they have a "disease"?

The medical model of calling drunkenness a "disease" leads many astray and away from the Cross. *No one needs forgiveness from God for a disease;* therefore, calling sin a disease does not lead people to the forgiveness of Christ. The truth will set you free and if you embrace the ideas of mankind that oppose the Holy Scriptures, you will imprison yourself to those ideas. Colossians 2:8 states: **"See to it that no one takes you captive by philosophy and empty deceit, according to human tradition, according to the elemental spirits of the world, and not according to Christ."** Do not allow the world's ideas to take you captive and keep you in bondage. Addiction and excessive use of a substance or activity is a sin problem that can be overcome by the power of Christ. No other power can overcome the sin of drunkenness and idolatry because it is God alone who changes the heart.

God's power within you only works when you agree with Him and His Word. God calls "addiction" a sin. You must call it sin, too. If you do not, you will wrongly lead your child to believe he is a victim of the man-made idea that addiction is a disease, when in reality it all begins with sinful choices. Mankind's idea that addiction is a disease began to be popularized in the 1930's. God and His Word have been around forever. I suggest that you agree with Him.

Because the Bible terms addiction as "idolatry," your child must understand that he is responsible for the choice to worship the idol of his choice. Help him to think responsibly about his choices to prevent him from developing a victim mentality. Simply point out the sinful desire in your child's heart, remind him that it is sin, and then pray with him to ask the Lord to forgive him of this sinful desire. Finally, pray with your child to ask God to give him His transforming power to enable him to replace the sinful choice with a godly choice in the future. The Lord's power to overcome idolatry and addiction is mighty, though it starts with humble prayer.

KEY IDEAS AND PRACTICAL THINGS TO DO

1. Write out Romans 12:17-21 and make a list of ways to plan to overcome someone else's wrong choices with good (i.e. prayer, kind word, thank you letter, etc.).

2. List ways you have "enabled" your child by either blame-shifting (excusing) your child's words and behaviors or by taking on their God-given responsibilities. Examples of some God-given responsibilities are to honor, respect, and obey parents in thoughts, words, and actions. If you as a parent have excused willful disobedience and not addressed your child's heart motives as sin, then you must repent to God and ask His forgiveness first. You may need to ask your children's forgiveness for this, too, and inform them that you are repenting to God by making the changes He requires in your actions in the future. (i.e., God holds your child accountable for her words to you; therefore, if she is disrespectful in how she answers you as a parent and a God-given authority of her, then you must address it as sin, administer appropriate discipline, call for your child to repent to God and to you,

and instruct your child to speak correctly and respectfully. It is a lot of work but your investment will go a long way.)

3. Evaluate your child's language in terms of the words you hear that foster thinking like a victim. Write down each time your child uses "victim" terminology and, next to each word / phrase, replace each with a biblical alternative that is truthful and acceptable. Ask a trusted Christian friend for help, if necessary.

Chapter 19
Be Responsible
(Obedient)

Both sets of parents for Matt and Raymond took an inactive role in their child's upbringing. Matt continued to abuse Adderall and Raymond continued to abuse alcohol and marijuana. Both boys went to college but Matt flunked out and took a job working as a waiter in a restaurant. Raymond made it through college, became an attorney, and makes a successful living in the eyes of the world eyes even though he smokes marijuana almost daily.

Since God holds your child and all of us responsible, the antidote to the victim mentality is to learn to be responsible and obedient to God. If he never learns to be responsible, your child will ultimately reject Christ by blaming God rather than himself for his problems. Most people who reject the Christian faith do so because they fail to take responsibility for their sins, or they fail to see their sins as their own fault.

The number one prayer of my heart is to see my children saved— for them to know God personally. I ask the Lord quite frequently to save their souls from hell by revealing who He is to them. I want them to have a relationship with Him. I know God is faithful to do His part. So what is my part in leading my children to Him?

One responsibility of mine is to teach them the Word of God and to share the Gospel, or Good News, with them. My children need to understand their great need for God's forgiveness and His great love to forgive sins through Jesus Christ. Therefore, my parental responsibility is to teach them in the everyday moments of life that God holds them responsible for their sins and that they are to prayerfully confess them and forsake them to find His mercy according to Proverbs 28:13: **"Whoever conceals his transgressions will not prosper, but he who confesses and forsakes them will obtain mercy."** Emphasizing a victim mentality only conceals a child's transgressions, which will not prosper my children.

What about you? If you allow your child to conceal his sin and think like a victim, he will eventually develop the darkened mind of a fool. Your child will be as a fool who says in his heart, **"There is no**

God" (Psalm 14:1). The Bible tells us there is a God who loves us and tells us His truth so that we might confess our sins and have life more abundantly. As a parent, you must hold your children accountable and foster their responsibility before a Holy God. God held both of His children, Adam and Eve, accountable for their sinful choices and you must do the same with your children. It is the duty of calling them to repentance, responsibility, and obedience.

Be a Biblical Counselor to Your Children

One of the most basic forms of biblical counseling is parenting. Children are constantly taking in information and sometimes making wrong conclusions. For example, one of my girls said, "Mommy, this sweater came in a Happy Meal®." My wife smiled and asked her what she meant by that statement knowing that she was given the sweater by friends of our family. My daughter responded by showing my wife the tag in her sweater that had a famous restaurant's tag sewn into it. My 8-year-old daughter wrongly concluded that the clothing must have come from the restaurant where they serve Happy Meals and not from a retail clothing store.

1 Corinthians 13:11 reminds us that children do not reason as adults: **"When I was a child, I spoke like a child, I thought like a child, I reasoned like a child. When I became a man, I gave up childish ways."** For this reason, children need parents to be biblical counselors who teach them what God says about the events in their lives so that they can be full of His wisdom and knowledge. In so doing, your children will learn how much they can trust Him at His Word. Their relationship with God will be strengthened by parents who learn the art of biblical counseling and asking good questions.

In the passage in Genesis 3, I once found it odd that the Lord asked four questions of Adam and Eve. Didn't God know all the answers? Isn't He omniscient? So why did God ask them questions? Were Adam and Eve so good at hiding that God couldn't find them?

I think you can guess that the questions were not for His information, but they were for the benefit of Adam and Eve to do some introspective thinking. God's questions were designed to make Adam and Eve think and be reflective. God knew where they were physically and spiritually. He wanted them to see for themselves how far they were from Him at that moment. God's questions rightly placed the responsibility of Adam and Eve's sinful choices upon themselves. God's questions were designed to lead them to confession and reconciliation with God.

In this same way, wise parents will ask their children questions when they observe or know that the child has deliberately disobeyed them. The purpose of the questions is to help the child see that his disobedience has led to the resulting consequence. This is the very thing that the Father God did for His children, Adam and Eve. He asked them four questions before He disciplined them with His divine consequences.

God's four questions move from general to specific. Each question becomes increasingly more intrusive, probing, and specific. Part of the reason for this shift from general to specific is due to Adam and Eve's blame-shifting responses. At first they failed to take full responsibility for their sinful choices; therefore, God was more specific with each question. God is so gracious!

Adam and Eve became aware of their nakedness before God because of their sinful choices. God had not changed. Mankind had changed because of sin. In the flesh, your child will automatically try to cover up his sinful choices. Expect it. However, do not allow the cover up to continue, but expose it with good questions like God asked of Adam and Eve.

In Genesis 3, Adam's response to his sin was sinful; so he was adding more sin to his situation. Adam blamed Eve, and then he even blamed God by saying, **"The woman whom you gave to be with me, she gave me fruit of the tree, and I ate."** In other words, "God, it's your fault because you gave Eve to me in the first place—without her existence, this would have never happened. She gave me the fruit. Ultimately, God, it's your fault." While it's true that Eve gave Adam the fruit, Adam knew better and he ate it. No one forced it down Adam's throat. Adam was acting in outright disobedience to God and His Word, yet he shifted the blame from himself to God and his wife. (I'm sure that some of you ladies are thinking: "Isn't that just like a man to throw his wife under the bus!")

Eve did not respond much better by saying, **"The serpent deceived me, and I ate."** Eve **"was deceived"** according to 1 Timothy 2:14, so she believed the lies of the serpent and disobeyed. To their credit, both Adam and Eve admitted their sinful choice at the end of each of their statements: "and I ate." However, before they admitted their sin, they deflected some of the blame toward others. They were not taking full responsibility though they did take part of it. Now, over six thousand years after this incident, substance abusers and "addicts" continue to use this oldest trick of the Book to shift the blame from themselves onto others or their circumstances. Some things never seem to change!

Adam and Eve were denying the truth of their reality. They had "messed up big time" by sinning against God. In His grace, He asked them questions so that they might come to a realization of the truth. If you master the art of asking questions as God did, you will lead your child to acknowledge the truth rather than deny it. The consequences should not change simply because your child takes responsibility. Some parents are so glad when their child admits to a sinful choice that they relieve the consequences completely. God did not do that for Adam and Eve, but He was gracious toward them. God allowed them to experience the consequences for their sin, and He is a perfect parent.

Asking Questions as God Would Ask Them

Most people do not know how to ask good questions because they are not good listeners. Many parents prefer lecturing to asking questions. Those parents want to be heard and understood rather than to hear and understand their children! The most critical skill I can teach parents in biblical counseling sessions is to ask questions like God did in Genesis 3. Parents often already acknowledge and see what is going on; however, their children do not. For this reason, good questions provoke the child to think by examining his own heart, which should lead him to see his sin and his great need for a Savior for those sins.

Here is a closer examination of those questions. Beginning in Genesis 3:9, God asked four questions of Adam and Eve. The first three are directed to Adam and the last one is to Eve. Here they are:

"Where are you?"

"Who told you that you were naked?"

"Have you eaten of the tree of which I commanded you not to eat?"

"What is this that you have done?"

The four questions are asked by God in this specific order for a purpose. God first asked Adam and Eve about their location. **"Where are you?"** is a question about their spiritual location as well as their physical location. Remember that they were physically hiding in the bushes and covered with fig leaves. God starts with the basics.

As parents, you can ask your children, "Where are you spiritually with the Lord right now?" after they have committed a sin. The child is not in a good place. Jesus said, **"If you love me, you will keep my commandments"** in John 14:15. In that moment when your child sinned, his love for Christ in that small moment of life was made visible when the child made a disobedient, unwise choice. Obedience to God is paramount in the Christian life because it demonstrates our love for Him and His great love to us. Anytime your child chooses to sin it demonstrates that at that moment, he loved himself more than he loved God and he was willing to act on it.

Again, if your child is already a follower of Jesus Christ, then his sinful choice simply means that in that moment he lived for pleasing himself rather than yielding to the power of the Holy Spirit. In that moment, he acted like an unbeliever rather than a believer and follower of Christ. In that moment, he chose to worship himself and to feed his own desire rather than to be obedient to God's Word. The anatomy of your child's sinful act is exactly the same as Adam and Eve's sinful act where a desire for a temporary pleasure outweighed a desire to please an eternal Father God. It was an act of love but not love for God—it was love for self.

The second question asked by the Lord is, **"Who told you that you were naked?"** Adam and Eve's nakedness was now their shame. They were unaware of their nakedness before their sinful disobedience. This question was designed to humble them and to demonstrate how they had believed the lies of Satan. In a way, God was showing them His true nature of integrity and honesty as compared to the deception and lies of Satan. Who are you listening to when you sin? You are listening to the voice of Satan and self. Ask your child: "When you sinned just now, were you thinking of yourself? Were you thinking of the one you hurt? Were you thinking of God when you did that?"

These questions are certainly convicting to a young child and that is precisely what needs to happen. The Holy Spirit convicts the world of sin for the good purpose of turning our hearts back to Christ according to Jesus in John 16:8: **"And when he comes, he will convict the world concerning sin and righteousness and judgment."** Conviction is productive because it brings our thoughts to acknowledge our sin and God's grace, which is the Gospel. The world and Satan tell us that God's conviction of our sins is not good and that we do not need to ever feel bad about one of our wrong choices, but God wants us to experience the freedom of forgiveness He grants to repentant sinners who acknowledge the truth.

The third question is **"Have you eaten of the tree of which I commanded you not to eat?"** Increasingly, God's questions are focusing more upon Adam's responsibility. Adam is now asked directly about what he has done. There is no way around this question. God's question is designed to bring confession, brokenness, humility, and repentance because God is ready to forgive them.

Ask your child a direct question at this point in your questioning (third question). For example, if your child hit his sister, then ask: "Have you hit your sister, which I told you not to do?" The desire here is to be more pointed in your question asking and to restate the rule of the home (or the command of God). If you are not sure what really happened, then ask him a more general question: "Have you sinned against someone, and you know it is wrong?" You can ask the question in different ways but I recommend you follow the model God has provided in His Word in Genesis 3.

The fourth and final question the Lord asked is **"What is this that you have done?"** This question was asked of Eve and is about as clear as any question ever asked. As a parent, ask your child to tell you what he or she has done. Children do not want to be forthcoming with confessions and will manipulate you and resist answering it in every way possible. You must hold them to the confession because that is what brings mercy according to Proverbs 28:13: **"Whoever conceals his transgressions will not prosper, but he who confesses and forsakes them will obtain mercy."** Your child needs the mercy of God. Ultimately, his sinful choice is against God and not just you, the parent. He may need to ask your forgiveness but he will *always* need to ask God's forgiveness—every time! Again, point him to God, his heavenly Father, and the Creator who forgives us of all our sins. Be sure to model this grace, mercy and forgiveness at the close of your confrontation. Hug your child and tell him you will now forget it.

Conclusion

Remember the fifth commandment: **"Honor your father and mother..."** This commandment places responsibility upon children to obey God by obeying their parents. There is no escape from responsibility. Alcohol and drug use, sexual sin, excessive shopping, gambling, cutting and self-injury, and all addictive behaviors do not provide an escape from our responsibility before God. Calling these things a disease or an illness does not change the reality that God holds us responsible for our thoughts, words, and actions. Asking questions and teaching your children the truth about their responsibility before the Lord for the glory of God and their benefit is the loving thing to do. Parents who are effective at addiction-proof parenting ask good questions of their children to illicit a response that brings the child back to a right relationship with God!

KEY IDEAS AND PRACTICAL THINGS TO DO

1. Write down the 4 questions of God mentioned in this chapter on a 3x5 card to keep handy so you can refer to it when interacting with your child in the future.

2. Make a list of your sins against your child. Help your child to make a list of his sins against you as a parent or guardian. Read Proverbs 28:13 and follow its counsel by confessing those sins to each other, asking for forgiveness, and then developing a practical plan of repentance to forsake the sins in the future.

3. Here's a challenge: Use the word "sin" and biblical words for "sin" (i.e. idolatry, stealing, lying, adultery, etc.) in your everyday conversations. Beware: You'll get funny looks from people because these words have been nearly eliminated from our culture and our language.

Chapter 19
The Perishing Mentality

After Derrick's death, his mother sought help for her grief from the church down the street from where she lived. Little did she know at that time, but the church offered biblical counseling free of charge. They showed her love and compassion and evangelized her with the Gospel so that she received forgiveness of her sin and freedom from her guilt. Derrick's mother repented of her sins of omission (failing to parent Derrick) and was reconciled to Christ through biblical counseling.

If your child is already displaying signs of addicted thinking or behavior, you are likely seeing the fourth mentality which is called a "perishing mentality." This mindset is opposite of what is portrayed in the following verses of Ephesians 5:19-20: **"...addressing one another in psalms and hymns and spiritual songs, singing and making melody to the Lord with all your heart, giving thanks always and for everything to God the Father in the name of our Lord Jesus Christ..."** A perishing mentality is defined as a "woe is me" attitude. It is an extreme manner of thinking that "bad things always happen to me." It is not reflective of a thankful heart. In children the thinking can be associated with statements such as, "All of my friends get to do that. I am the only one who can't do it." The character, Eeyore, from Winnie the Pooh comes to mind.

Proverbs 31:6-7 are verses that reflect a perishing mentality: **"Give strong drink to the one who is perishing, and wine to those in bitter distress; let them drink and forget their poverty and remember their misery no more."** Someone who is dying on his deathbed due to some illness is given strong medications (drink) to allow him to forget his condition. This person is likely in agonizing pain and needs relief. In these cases, the Bible gives the directive to use strong wine (which is a drug in liquid form, please remember) to assist this person. God is very gracious by giving us these verses to direct our thinking about physical pain and suffering.

However, the addict suffers from emotional pain and has developed a perishing mentality though there often is not physical pain.[50] The Bible refers to the truth that a "crushed spirit" (or a wounded spirit from emotional hurts) is more difficult to bear than physical pain in Proverbs 18:14: **"A man's spirit will endure sickness, but a crushed spirit who can bear?"** Emotional hurts can overwhelm any of us. It is for this reason that self-help groups say that the "number one offender" for a drunkard is resentment. Resentments develop when one re-feels the hurt experienced before. It is like ripping the scab off of a wound that is healing—the pain comes back when that wound is re-opened. This opening of the wound brings bitterness as one is resentful and re-feeling all of the emotions of the past. Children should not be allowed to dwell on hurt feelings and emotional pain derived from perceived injustices. It is important for parents to recognize these "perishing" statements when they come up and expose them for the sinful and detrimental thoughts they are.

The perishing mentality is a destructive way of thinking and develops in two ways. First, when a person focuses upon past hurts so much that those hurts begin to be the center of their universe, a perishing mentality quickly develops. Jesus Christ must be the center of our life, not other people's wrongdoing. That is a wrong response to being wronged! 1 Thessalonians 5:15 states: **"See that no one repays anyone evil for evil, but always seek to do good to one another and to everyone."** You must realize the importance of teaching your child to have a forgiving spirit toward those wounds that he will experience. The child may not be able to personally forgive the other person but he must focus his thoughts on Christ to develop an attitude of forgiveness. Ephesians 4:32 reminds us to treat others as we have been treated by the Lord: **"Be kind to one another, tenderhearted, forgiving one another, as God in Christ forgave you."**

Second, when a person focuses on what he does not have rather than what he does possess eternally in Christ, a perishing mentality develops. It is a sinful way to think, especially when one has been given eternal life through the forgiveness of Christ. It is a sinful way to think because it demonstrates ingratitude. The perishing mentality is mired in self-pity. Self-pity is prideful because it involves too much

---

[50] Some people get hooked on prescription pain killers they have been given for physical pain, but have now found non-physical reasons for taking more medicine. God looks at the heart and the motives for taking the medications.

focus upon self and what we are not getting. It is based upon the thought that "I am not getting what I deserve and I deserve a whole lot better than what I am getting." The truth is that God is very gracious to us since we all deserve eternal punishment in hell for our sins. However, by the grace of God and His justice in punishing Jesus, we are forgiven and spared from what we really deserve.

Those enslaved to addiction have a warped view of what they think they deserve.[51] They do not understand that God's grace has been extended to them in every area of their lives. This way of thinking breeds deep resentments which often feed addictive behavior. As a parent, you must foster the following biblical concept in your child's mind: "I deserve worse than what I am getting and I am thankful for God's grace and mercy." Mercy is not getting what you deserve. Grace is getting what you do not deserve. Both mercy and grace are unmerited and unearned. One receives these gifts from God through the sacrifice of the Lord Jesus Christ.

Repentance from sins is also a gift from God. It is the kindness and patience of God that should lead us to repentance according to Romans 2:4: **"Or do you presume on the riches of his kindness and forbearance and patience, not knowing that God's kindness is meant to lead you to repentance?"** Repentance is turning away from sinful practices and turning toward God; it is living God's way in obedience to Him and fills us with all kinds of spiritual blessings. Repentance is good and yields good fruit. Encourage your children to repent from their sins and teach repentance as the blessing that it truly is.[52]

Children who develop a perishing mentality say things like:

"Why do all of the bad things happen to me?"

"Why is God punishing me?"

"Why can't I have more money (or material possessions)?"

"My car is nice but yours is nicer." (discontentment)

"Woe is me!"

"Why do I have to be an addict?" (which is also the victim

---

[51] Here is the connection between an entitlement, consumer, and a perishing mentality. All of these mindsets breed resentment.

[52] For some reason, some Christians think of repentance as a bad thing but nothing could be further from the truth. For one thing, repentance brings freedom from guilt.

mentality because it is a failure to take responsibility. The word "addict" should be replaced with "drunkard" or "idolater" which places the responsibility upon the person).

Note all of the "why" questions. "Why" questions should rarely, if ever, be asked of God because they question His goodness, love, and sovereignty. Do not "shake your fist" at God and ask "why" questions. Only ask Him *what* He wants to teach you through the trials of your life. James 1:2-3 states: **Count it all joy, my brothers, when you meet trials of various kinds, for you know that the testing of your faith produces steadfastness.** Here again in these verses, you see the importance of having a joyful mentality based upon the loving character of God and not upon your circumstances. If you want to ask a "why" question of our gracious Father in heaven, then ask, "Why do you bless me so much when you know all of my sinful thoughts and choices I made yesterday and in my past?"

Parents who unwittingly encourage the perishing mentality in their children make statements like:

"I know you have it harder than others, my child."

"School is harder for you than it is for your brother." Comparisons with other children breed the perishing mentality. Always compare your child with himself in the past and not with other children.

"If you get bored and have nothing to do, come see me." The parent is full of self-pity and displaying it for the child.

"We cannot do that because we don't have the money. God will have to provide better."

"We aren't as blessed as your friend's family."

"You just are not as smart as your sister."

"You are stupid and will never amount to anything."

For any addict, the focus of the perishing mentality is upon self. This self-centered focus shrinks one's world down to one person: me. Me, myself, and I are the only persons that the addict and idolater is concerned about pleasing. That "one person world" is a lonely place to be because few people want to join in a world that is consumed with self since the wrong person is king! Relationships are always "give and take" and the self-centered person with a perishing mentality will have very few real friendships because others will grow weary of his attitude and lack of interest in others.

Conclusion

God is more concerned about your child's holiness than He is with his happiness. In other words, focus upon teaching your child to have the correct, biblical mindset which will set him apart from the lies and patterned thinking of this world (Romans 12:2). Then, when he learns to do what God requires and to think with a grateful mentality, he will become "holy," which means "set apart" and different, as God is different from us. Isaiah 55:8-9 reminds us of God's holiness and how different He is from us because of our sinful nature: **"For my thoughts are not your thoughts, neither are your ways my ways, declares the Lord. For as the heavens are higher than the earth, so are my ways higher than your ways and my thoughts than your thoughts."**

The goal is to think and act like Jesus and to teach that to your children. In time, your child will trust God more, be more stable emotionally, and enjoy the happiness produced by living a holy life. Holiness is the primary goal and it often produces the fruit of true joy that comes from the Holy Spirit. Do not allow your children to be ungrateful or to have a perishing mentality. Foster a grateful heart in you child by pointing him to the goodness of God in all things.

KEY IDEAS AND PRACTICAL THINGS TO DO

1. Put a nickel into a jar each time a member of your family says something described in this chapter, sarcastically, hurtful to others or in a negative tone of voice in a perishing manner.

2. Replace perishing words with words which are grateful, joyful, and glorifying to God. Write examples of these words and phrases on a 3x5 note card.

3. List ten thoughts that you have had in the past that triggered your emotions and actions to respond. List both good and bad examples.

Chapter 21
Be Grateful(Joy)

It is now ten years after Derrick's death. His mother is teaching younger women to love their children by being active, biblical parents who discipline consistently and lovingly. The Lord has been gracious to her by allowing her to remarry a godly man and to raise two children with her new husband. Both of these children are walking with the Lord Jesus in an intimate relationship and she is grateful to have been an instrument of righteousness in the Hands of Christ.

A perishing mentality can be replaced by a joyful mentality of gratitude according to Ephesians 5:18-20: **"And do not get drunk with wine, for that is debauchery, but be filled with the Spirit, addressing one another in psalms and hymns and spiritual songs, singing and making melody to the Lord with all your heart, <u>giving thanks always and for everything</u> to God the Father in the name of our Lord Jesus Christ…"** (emphasis mine). Do you realize that the verse is in the context of the command "do not get drunk with wine"? God knows that the heart of someone desiring to be drunk with wine is often ungrateful. If you fail to cultivate a grateful heart in your child, then you may be unknowingly leading him to have unthankful thinking that may lead him one day to choosing drunkenness.

Therefore, as a parent, you must model a thankful heart before your children because that will foster an attitude of gratitude in your children. Verbalizing thankfulness for all things demonstrates that you trust God! You may not realize it, but being grateful to God even for the difficulties in your life shows your child that you trust the Lord. I remember reading an excellent illustration of this in Jay Younts' book, *Everyday Talk*, where a Christian father planned to play golf, looked out the window, and yelled, "Stupid rain!" in front of his child. According to Jay Younts, the message to the child was that God's plan was not as good as the father's plan (Proverbs 3:5-8; Proverbs 28:26).[53]

Children are not born with thankful hearts. In fact, just the opposite is true. Because of the obvious limitations, babies think only of their own needs to be fed, to be loved, and to be dry and

---

[53] Younts, Jay A., *Everyday Talk,* Shepherd Press, Wapwallopen, PA, pp. 15-16.

warm. They typically respond in one of two ways to how these needs are met: smiling or crying. It is the very beginning of the entitlement mentality, and it is from here that parents must train them to be satisfied with their lives and recognize their blessings. It is when children are old enough to make a comparative observation of what they have in material goods and what others enjoy that they begin to develop the victim and perishing mentalities. We have considered some of the thoughts associated with these mentalities. Now let us look at how we, as parents, can foster an attitude of gratitude in our children.

Be on guard against unrealistic expectations. Children and adults alike often make plans with a great sense of optimism only to find that things didn't go as they had hoped or expected. Unrealistic expectations can lead to many disappointments and disappointments lead to perishing and victim thinking. For people in various addictions, childhood expectations carry over into adulthood. Holidays, for example, were exciting, carefree and full of joy. But as adults, we cannot capture those feelings and for some, people holidays become sad days, and many try to replace the sadness with sinful idolatry.

Galatians 5:22-23 tells us of the fruit of the Spirit produced in a surrendered Christian's life: **"But the fruit of the Spirit is love, joy, peace, patience, kindness, goodness, faithfulness, gentleness, self-control; against such things there is no law."** God wants to work through Christians by His Spirit to produce His fruit. When you teach your children to be responsible and obedient to the will of Christ, then they will exhibit the fruit of the Spirit. One fruit of the Spirit is joy. According to Ephesians 5:19, joy is expressed in words to others that will sound like music to their ears: **"addressing one another in psalms and hymns and spiritual songs."** In other words, when someone has the spiritual fruit of joy, his words will be full of gratitude and thankfulness.

In fact, verse 19 goes on to say that a grateful heart will continue to be directed to God as **"singing and making melody to the Lord with all your heart."** **"Out of the abundance of the heart, his mouth speaks"** is what Jesus says a person's words reveal (Luke 6:45). Words reveal the attitudes and thoughts of the heart. Therefore, a transforming drunkard will talk to others with an attitude of gratitude as their hearts are singing with thankfulness to Christ.

Parents must encourage thankfulness in their children. For example, a child that is given a toy should say "thank you" to the giver of the gift. Not only is that good manners but it is an expression of gratitude. Teach your child to say "thank you" even if he does not like the toy he is being given. A simple acknowledgment is not lying or hypocritical since the child can give the gift to a younger sibling, a cousin, a friend, or a less fortunate child. Then the child can be thankful that he has something to give others or could be thankful that this person thought of them, or for a number of other reasons. Train your child to be thankful for all things.

As a young Christian, I was always thankful for the personal green 'traffic' lights in my life. As long as God kept the traffic lights green, I would exuberantly say things like "I praise You, Lord" and "Thank you, Jesus!" However, I was not always thankful for the red lights in my life. If I came to what was perceived as a red light, I sang a different tune: "Where are you, now, Lord?" and "Why, Lord? Why me?" My theology was that everything I thought was good was from the Lord and everything I thought was bad was either from Satan or that God was not pleased with me. Now, as a mature believer in Christ, I praise God for both the green lights and the red lights in my life. I may not be as enthusiastic for the red lights but I have learned to see God's goodness and to trust His plan more than I trust my own, puny perspective.

In addition to teaching your children to thankfulness, teach them to trust God even when they experience red lights in their lives. Do so first by modeling thankfulness for your own personal disappointments. Children learn more from parents by observation than by listening to what parents tell them to do. Your children will see and hear your response to those difficulties and they will model you. Then, when their red lights come, teach them not to act as though something bad was happening and God was not involved. Teach them that their thoughts about their circumstances are not to be trusted more than God's sovereignty, according to Proverbs 3:5-8: **"Trust in the Lord with all your heart, and do not lean on your own understanding. In all your ways acknowledge him, and he will make straight your paths. Be not wise in your own eyes; fear the Lord, and turn away from evil. It will be healing to your flesh and refreshment to your bones."**

As a parent, you must instill biblical thinking and principles in your child. The child will not think biblically by osmosis; a practical, real-life teaching example is best. Sadly, the vast majority of addicts I am privileged to counsel exhibit *unthankful* hearts. Many of them are far more blessed than children in poverty-stricken areas but they wrongly view their circumstances. Just as many people wrongly think they are true victims, many addicts believe they are not blessed by God though they may have an abundance of material wealth, spiritual gifts, abilities, and the like. It truly is an amazing deception.

For children and adults alike, a perishing mentality must be replaced with what I call a joyful, or grateful, mentality, because I want to emphasize that joy is a purposeful manner of thinking fueled by a thankful heart. According to Ephesians 5:20, **"giving thanks always and for everything to God the Father in the name of our Lord Jesus Christ"** is a key for preventing any type of "addiction." Children must learn to give thanks always and for everything.

In a radio interview a Christian quarterback was asked: "Why don't you praise the Lord on your knees every time you throw a touchdown pass?" The reporter was referencing the actions of a rival quarterback who also was a Christian. The implication was that since both of these men were Christian quarterbacks, why was there a difference in their celebration of a touchdown pass? The first quarterback responded: "I could get down on my knees to pray and thank the Lord for every touchdown I throw, but then my Bible tells me to 'give thanks always and for everything to God' so I would also need to get down on my knees and thank God for the interceptions I throw. And my coach would not like it if I didn't try to tackle the guy who caught my interception; I want to play!"

I thought this man made a great point: we are to thank God for both the touchdowns and the interceptions in our lives! Mature Christians learn to thank God even for the interceptions of life because they understand that a redemptive God will work all things together for the Christian's good. Teach your child to thank God for the interceptions, failures, and wrong choices in his life though there may be negative consequences. Help your child to see that God will redeem those failures for His glory and your child's benefit. There are always lessons to grow us spiritually no matter how many times we fall!

Being Intentionally Joyful

The word "happy" comes from the word "happenstance." Like the word "circumstance," "happenstance" simply refers to the circumstances of life that tend to make us happy when they are positive and sad when the circumstances are negative. As Christians, we are not to live in this roller-coaster manner that is dependent upon our life situations. When people live this way, they develop a victim mentality because they think they are merely a product of the circumstance of their environment. The reality is that people with grateful, thankful hearts are happier people. As Christians, we are to live more purposefully according to Colossians 3:2: **"Set your minds on things that are above, not on things that are on earth."**

We are not to deny that sometimes bad things happen and pretend nothing is wrong. On the contrary, Romans 12:15 states: **"Rejoice with those who rejoice, weep with those who weep."** Acknowledge the hurt and bad occurrences in this world, but do not dwell on it. Forgive in your heart and **"turn the other cheek"** (Matthew 5:39; Luke 6:29). Then, focus your thinking upon the good things in your life, and the character and power of God to be redemptive in your situation. An amazing attribute of God is His redemption in that He makes our bad, sinful choices and circumstances into good for us and for His own glory. Only the Lord can turn sin into something that saves our lives just as He did for Joseph's brothers in Genesis 37 & 47. How awesome is our God and worthy to be praised!

So many of those enslaved to all types of addiction have a perishing mentality because they are operating in the flesh. The replacement for that mentality is the intentional joyful mentality of gratitude. I have found that most addicts are led by their emotions. They choose feelings over obedience. Teach your child *not* to make rash, emotional decisions but decisions based upon the unchanging Word of God. Emotions change quickly. God and His Word never change. *Emotions change when one's thinking changes.* Teach your child to change his thinking about his situation. Help him to see the good in the situation and positive emotions will follow. Thoughts come first, and then emotions follow.

Mankind is made in the image of God with an intellect, emotions, and a will. Actions chosen by our will also lead to emotions. Emotions have the power for good or evil. For example, when we make the right choices, emotions of joy follow. On the other hand, when we makes wrong choices that disobey a Holy God, then emotions of depression, sadness, anger, or fear occur. Those emotions resulting from our sinful choices are designed to bring us to confession and repentance with Christ, but many people try to medicate or change the emotional state rather than deal with it biblically.

Conclusion

Contentment is learned according to Philippians 4:9: **"What you have learned and received and heard and seen in me—practice these things, and the God of peace will be with you."** Your child will learn by modeling you—whether good or bad. What things is Paul referring to? In the verses preceding verse 9, Paul tells the church at Philippi to rejoice in the Lord, to not be anxious but to pray, to ask God for what is needed, to trust God, to focus on thoughts that are true, pure, and praiseworthy, and now to model Paul who had learned contentment. You must instill these biblical values in your child's thoughts early in life.

Teaching your child how to think biblically produces joyful thinking, emotions, and actions by the power of the Holy Spirit. Philippians 4:8 tells you to focus your thoughts upon the right things. God knows our emotions will follow our thoughts. If we only focus upon evil, then we will think that evil is winning, but in reality Jesus has made Satan a defeated foe. Though we live in a fallen world cursed by man's sin, we must focus our eyes upon the Victor, the Lord Jesus Christ. Teach your child to focus upon his relationship with Christ by cultivating a grateful heart, which is the manifestation of a joyful mentality. This is the key to overcoming all addictions and it is how to avoid them as well.

KEY IDEAS AND PRACTICAL THINGS TO DO

1. List the things that the Lord has given you for which you can be thankful. Help your child to make a list, too.

2. For a week, focus upon helping your child to be thankful for both the good and the "bad" things in his/her life circumstances according to Romans 8:28.

3. Discuss Philippians 4:8 with your child and together come up with examples of whatever is true, honorable, just, pure, lovely, commendable, excellent and worthy of praise.

Chapter 22
The Rebellious Mentality

As an adult now with her own family, Edna recognizes the importance of spending time in relationship with her children. She knew her parents loved her, but she never felt close and connected to them. She feared them, but that fear never kept her from making poor choices. Though she only tried marijuana that one time, she paid a heavy price for it. When she was younger she struggled with an eating "addiction." She would battle overeating, and sometimes purging, for many years until she sought help from her pastor and his wife.

God wants us to have a Christlike submissive spirit, but our flesh fights against that with a "rebellious mentality." This is the fifth and final mentality of addictive thinking. Those who are rebellious to the Lord and to the human authorities He places over them act independently and desire to be self-sufficient. In reality, only God is self-sufficient and all human beings are dependent upon Him and others for help. Human beings are fallen creatures who are born needy, dependent, insufficient, and weak. Worldly thinking finds these qualities to be offensive, but they must be embraced because committed followers of Christ understand that they need the Lord, and are dependent upon the Lord and others. We must find sufficiency only in Christ, and rely upon the strength of the Holy Spirit. Self-sufficiency is not the goal of Christianity.

When a person has a neuromuscular disease of some sort, the head (brain and neurological system) no longer controls the hands and other parts of the body. The body of Christ often functions as if it has a similar disease and this must not be so! Jesus said in John 15:5, **"I am the vine and you are the branches...apart from me you can do nothing."** The body of Christ must submit its "limbs" to the Head and not act independently of Him. True followers of Christ are submitted to Him and His human authorities, and they value the protection and love that submission provides.

When I am counseling addicts in various "addictions" I find that many of them have a rebellious spirit. They don't want to be submissive to any authority and they want to be in complete control of their lives. We see these attitudes begin to manifest in young children who want to have their own way in their interactions with parents, siblings and friends. "I'll do it!" "I want it!" "Give it to me!" are all demands we hear from them. To deny their request is to provoke angry outbursts. Unless parents determine a biblical response to these demands and outbursts, the child will become an 'out of control teen-ager who causes fights and quarrels in the family. James 4:1 says, **"What causes quarrels and what causes fights among you? Is it not this, that your passions are at war within you? You desire and do not have…"**

The typical desire of a child's heart is to be his own boss. They often act out of emotion; as though they are God and God Himself does not exist. There is no fear of the Lord. Proverbs 1:7 reminds us that **"the fear of the Lord is the beginning of knowledge; fools despise wisdom and instruction."** What is a "fool" according to the Bible? A fool is a rebel at heart. There are many, many proverbs about the fool and rebellion is the underlying theme in nearly all of them. Fools are not dumb. In fact, many fools are brilliant people in an intellectual sense. When you think of a fool, you might think of someone who is stupid or ignorant, but that is not what a biblical fool is. A biblical fool is someone who lives as though there is no God and as if he is a god. Fools act independently of God and are not submissive to human authorities.

Fools get fired from jobs because of their unwillingness to do things according to their employer's rules, not because they are incompetent. Fools cause havoc in the church because of their lack of submission to God's Word and the pastors who care for them. Fools end up alone or with very few friends because they are self-centered and selfish.

Think of all of the mentalities that have preceded the rebellious mentality. First, you have a child who thinks he is entitled to have everything he wants in life. "It's my right," he mistakenly thinks. Then he consumes everything he wants and gets in life for selfish pleasure. He becomes frustrated when he fails to get what he wants and he either blames others including God or he believes it is entirely his fault. Both of these extremes of thinking are fixated upon him and lead him to believe he is a powerless victim. Feeling powerless, angry, hurt, bitter, or fearful, the child now has a perishing outlook toward life that "anything that can go wrong will go wrong and usually does go wrong for me." This child's focus remains upon himself and he becomes mired in self-pity.

At this stage of his life, who does he trust the most? The answer is himself. Even if he thinks everything is completely his fault, he wrongly concludes that since it must be his fault that he is in this situation, then he alone must be the one to pull himself out of it. He trusts in himself not God. If he thinks his problems are the fault of others, then he will become more angry and bitter and will certainly not turn to anyone else for help since no one else can be trusted. At this point, this child is not yet completely broken and will simply rely upon himself and no one else. He is officially a rebel and a "fool" biblically speaking.

Rebellion

Discipline is extremely vital to combat the rebellious mentality in children. It bears repeating that discipline is essential for learning to occur. Children who are "spoiled" by their parents often end up being addicts. Do not ruin your children by giving them everything they want. Suffering and doing without can be good teaching tools. Obviously, you can be too extreme by being too harsh with your children, but most parents err on the other side of this extreme.

Parents who give their children too many choices and too much power foster a rebellious mentality in their children. These parents make comments and ask questions like:

"Do you want to wear the blue outfit or the yellow outfit?"

"Where would you like to eat?" The question in and of itself is fine; however, a four year-old's preference should not determine where the family eats. Let the parent, especially the father, make the decision to teach the child about authority.

"Eat the carrots and then you may have ice cream." Bargaining with your child in this manner is manipulation. The child is often in control when this statement is made.

"You can do whatever you want to do."

"You can do whatever you want when you want." Though not often stated in this way, this message is often conveyed to a child in other words by parents.

"You do not have to obey that teacher."

"You do not have to follow this rule."

"Let's go ahead and buy this and not tell Daddy."

"Don't tell Mommy that I let you do this."

"I will let you watch this TV show but don't tell your parents." (Said by a grandparent.)

Some parents foster a rebellious mentality in their children by neglecting their God-given duty to raise their children to love and glorify God. The church is not primarily responsible for the spiritual rearing of children, though some parents mistakenly think so. The church's duty is to equip parents to train their children spiritually. Parents are primarily responsible for the spiritual and physical development of their children.

A sad proverb that emphasizes the extreme of neglecting a child is Proverbs 22:6: **"Train up a child in the way he should go; even when he is old he will not depart from it."** As a parent, it is your duty to teach your child the right direction to go. If you neglect that duty, then your child will raise himself and learn to be his own authority. Children need their parents' interpretation of events as long as that interpretation agrees with the Bible. When a parent is neglectful, a child makes his own interpretations and becomes his own authority. As the child grows older, he will very likely not depart from being his own authority. It will be difficult for the neglected child to submit to authorities as an adult. Many of these children develop a rebellious mentality that often leads to a period of addiction.

Servant-Minded

Jesus, who is God, had the right to be king, yet He came to serve us. He did not come to be served since He gave His life as a ransom for the salvation of many according to Matthew 20:25-28: **"But Jesus called them to him and said, 'You know that the rulers of the Gentiles lord it over them, and their great ones exercise authority over them. It shall not be so among you. But whoever would be great among you must be your servant, and whoever would be first among you must be your slave, even as the Son of Man came not to be served but to serve, and to give his life as a ransom for many.'"** On the contrary, rebels do not serve anyone else unless it profits them. They often do not love unconditionally and do not have a servant's mindset, which was the mind of Christ in these verses above.

Pride is the hindrance to being servant-minded as it feeds a rebel's heart. When a home revolves around a child, as though he is the center of the family's universe, the child will develop rebel-like characteristics, which will only manifest when he does not get his way. That is when you will see temper tantrums that occur no matter what the age of a child—even adult-aged children will use temper tantrums, "guilt trips," and manipulation ploys to get their way.

To avoid the rebellious mentality and to foster servant-mindedness, it is recommended that your home not be centered on your children or their activities, i.e., ballet, baseball, football, and the like. Also, do not include your children in parental decision-making in your home, but ask them to leave the room while you discuss important matters with your spouse. If you are not married, discuss these matters with a trusted Christian friend or pastor, but do NOT include your child in adult decision-making for that may provoke your child to anger by promoting him to a position like that of a spouse. Though the child is not a spouse, some divorced parents turn to an older sibling to share their lives and to ask for opinions and input on decisions. This is a role they do not want. It will only confuse and provoke feelings of anger, especially when you demote your child from "spouse-status" back to "child-status." It would be like a demotion at a job![54]

One way to promote servant-mindedness in your home is to offer opportunities for one child to serve another. When one of your children does not have a fork at the kitchen table, for example, ask for a volunteer to go get a fork for that child. It gives one child an opportunity to serve another and it teaches some valuable lessons. First, it values the sibling. Second, it is sacrificial, which is how Christ Jesus lived His life. Third, it is serving others and not being served. For the child who did not have a fork, a lesson is that the child is not to be independent, self-reliant, and self-sufficient. Sometimes, we need the help of others. While we do want our children to know how to take care of themselves, we want them to learn to rely upon others and to receive service. We also use the opportunity to point out how easy it is to think of others and serve them, no matter how small you are.

Children must be taught to submit to the authorities that God has placed over them even if they seem to be harsh or unfair.

---

[54] This is frequently why remarriages and subsequent blended families initially have severe problems. A parent has a new spouse and the child is "demoted" in the family as the parent now turns to the new spouse for intimacy. The child resents the lack of intimacy with the parent that never should have occurred in the first place.

1 Peter 2:18-19 commands followers of Christ to do just that and gives the reason why: **"Servants, be subject to your masters with all respect, not only to the good and gentle but also to the unjust. For this is a gracious thing, when, mindful of God, one endures sorrows while suffering unjustly."** God is not telling us to submit to sin, but that He is honored when we respect authorities who are unjust, because He put them there. Children who can submit to unjust employers, parents, and other authorities will please the Lord and reap the benefits of that submissive spirit. 1 Peter 2:13-15 commands Christians: **"Be subject for the Lord's sake to every human institution, whether it be to the emperor as supreme, or to governors as sent by him to punish those who do evil and to praise those who do good. For this is the will of God, that by doing good you should put to silence the ignorance of foolish people."** It is the will of God for you to be submissive to those who are in authority, even if they act foolishly and wrongfully. In other words, by honoring the authority structure that is in place, one can submit to unjust rulers and allow the Lord to silence them by His power.

It is painful to see your child treated unfairly in sports, band, school clubs, friendships, and other social areas. However, rather than allow him to quit because of the unfair treatment, teach him to do what is right in the Lord's eyes through this trial in life. They will see that God honors those who honor Him and His authority structure. Allowing your child to quit may temporarily fix the problem, but a greater lesson is at stake here, for God's glory and your child's good.

Conclusion

Addiction-proof parenting is not easy. Teaching your child to submit to flawed authorities is a challenge for you as a parent and for your child as well.[55] However, the outcome of pleasing God and glorifying God is worth it. Your child will learn to be a servant and not a rebel. In so doing, God will reward your obedience to Him and your mindset to please Him. Make your primary goal to please Him alone and not your child or anyone else. When you and your

---

[55] Again, we are not talking about sinfully abusive authorities or being a pacifist. Teach your child to stand for what is right, but if there is no sin or abuse, teach your child to submit to the authority God has placed over him/her as unto the Lord. It's an act of worship.

child seek to please God, the rebellious mentality will be powerfully overcome and be replaced with a spirit of submissiveness to the Lord.

KEY IDEAS AND PRACTICAL THINGS TO DO

1. Read and write out Psalm 14:1 and Proverbs 1:7 during a family devotional time to discuss with your child the importance of thinking properly about God's rightful place in your lives.

2. Do a word study on "fool" just in the book of Proverbs alone and discuss with your child each one daily. Have your child evaluate each one of these and to confess failures when appropriate in order to ask forgiveness.

3. Write out several examples in your life when you had a harsh boss or someone in authority over you. Tell your child how this experience has shaped your life for the best.

Chapter 23
Be Submissive

Edna's children grew strong in their Christian faith. They learned how to think biblically through both of their parents' strong teaching of God's Word and their parents' faithful commitment to live according to these biblical principles. Their relationship with their parents was unique because they felt free to tell their parents anything, even about their sinful choices, and they would still be accepted and loved even though they knew they must still face the consequences of their choices. Their faith in Christ was real, relational, and thriving as they passed on their faith to their children.

The idea of "submission" is a foreign concept for many people today. God is our ultimate authority; we are to submit our wills to His. God places human beings in places of authority over us and we are to submit to them. This authority begins in the home with the parents who are to enforce God's rules using the rod and reproof. The authority continues at the workplace where a boss is in authority over an employee and has the power to discipline and terminate him from the job. God has also placed the government as an authority over mankind with the power of the sword to enforce God's laws. Finally, the church has God-given authority over the body of believers with the power to exercise church discipline for the purpose of calling a sinning believer to repentance and right relationship with Christ.

Everywhere you look there is authority. God commands us to submit to Him in the First Commandment: **"You shall have no other gods before Me"** (Exodus 20:3). Then, authority is emphasized on a human level as it begins in the home according to the Fifth Commandment: **"Honor your father and mother..."** (Exodus 20:12). The idea of submission is an essential concept for the betterment of society and the betterment of human beings. Persons who fail to submit end up injured in the hospital, imprisoned in jail, or dead in the grave. Submission is a concept that you must teach your child or your headaches will be numerous. The mentality of rebellion is less likely in a child who has learned the contentment of submission to God and the authorities in his life.

Submission is the Heart of Christ

Submission is a simple concept, but simple does not mean easy to put into practice. Why? It is because our flesh fights against the Holy Spirit that dwells within us. Romans 7:21-25 explains this internal war: **"So I find it to be a law that when I want to do right, evil lies close at hand. For I delight in the law of God, in my inner being, but I see in my members another law waging war against the law of my mind and making me captive to the law of sin that dwells in my members. Wretched man that I am! Who will deliver me from this body of death? Thanks be to God through Jesus Christ our Lord! So then, I myself serve the law of God with my mind, but with my flesh I serve the law of sin."** One of these internal wars has to do with your will and submission.

In the flesh, a person wants to be self-reliant, independent, and strong in their own strength. "I want to do whatever I want to do whenever I want to do it." In the flesh, a person wants to serve his own desires. "If it feels good, then do it" is a worldly lie that feeds the flesh. If taken too far, this idea of doing what feels good will lead our society to even greater problems than it is facing today. People are already doing what they please, leading them to be self-centered and sinful by committing sexual sins, murder, robbery, and the like. If some people do what they feel like doing, then other people are going to get hurt.

The biblical principle of not doing what you feel like but doing what God commands is essential to having a healthy relationship with God, spouse, children, friends, church family members, extended family, and co-workers. We must all learn to say "no" to the flesh and to say "yes" to the Holy Spirit. The Spirit-filled life takes twice the amount of effort for this very reason. The Lord Jesus illustrated this point well in Matthew 26:39-44:

> **And going a little farther he fell on his face and prayed, saying, "My Father, if it be possible, let this cup pass from me; nevertheless, not as I will, but as you will." And he came to the disciples and found them sleeping. And he said to Peter, "So, could you not watch with me one hour? Watch and pray that you may not enter into temptation. The spirit indeed is willing, but the flesh is weak." Again, for the second time, he went away and prayed, "My**

Father, if this cannot pass unless I drink it, your will be done." And again he came and found them sleeping, for their eyes were heavy. So, leaving them again, he went away and prayed for the third time, saying the same words again. Then he came to the disciples and said to them, "Sleep and take your rest later on. See, the hour is at hand, and the Son of Man is betrayed into the hands of sinners. Rise, let us be going; see, my betrayer is at hand."

Jesus prayed three times asking the Father to remove from Him the heavy burden of going to the cross and being separated from the Father. As a Man, that was Jesus' will as a human being. Nevertheless, Jesus submitted to the will of the Father each time. In verse 39, He said, **"Not as I will, but as You will,"** and that is the lesson of submission demonstrated by our Lord in a clear, real historical event. Jesus said **"Your will be done"** again in verse 43.

Hebrews 5:7-10 relates this very event to us: **"In the days of his flesh, Jesus offered up prayers and supplications, with loud cries and tears, to him who was able to save him from death, and he was heard because of his reverence. Although he was a son, he learned obedience through what he suffered. And being made perfect, he became the source of eternal salvation to all who obey him, being designated by God a high priest after the order of Melchizedek."** Verse 8 says Jesus "learned obedience through what He suffered." If Jesus trusted the Father and learned obedience and He was perfect, how much more must we trust the Father and learn obedience through our suffering?

One such teenager named Dave never learned submission, and he experienced harsh consequences as a result. Dave would ignore his parent's advice, his teacher's advice, and his pastor's advice. He was a young man who submitted to no one. Dave had to learn things the "hard way" by experience. For example, his father told him not to ride his bike on a dangerous mountain road but Dave did it anyway. The result could have been disastrous as he lost control riding down the hill and almost went over a rocky ledge, but he was able to hop off of his bike in time. Needless to say, he lost his bike and injured his leg severely.

Dave never learned the beautiful protection of submission that would spare him from physical pain and consequences. Dave ignored both his teacher's advice and his pastor's biblical counsel from 1 Corinthians 15:33 to avoid a particular group of friends at school when they discovered those kids were involved with alcohol and drugs. Dave experienced the spiritual consequences of his choice to ignore this advice and biblical wisdom, and it eventually led him away from the Lord to a life of drug-dealing and despair.

Teach your child that submission is the "willful placement of oneself under an authority." Submission means to "yield oneself to the will of another."[56] It can also be called "surrender." Isn't that what God calls all followers of Christ to do: surrender? Although she did not always, my wife now embraces this word as my **"helper suitable"** (Genesis 2:18) and thinks of it in simple terms. She remembers what this means practically by thinking that "sub" means "under" and that "mission" means one's purpose. She values her mission to be my helper suitable and that one of her primary purposes in life is to help me. Without my wife's submissive spirit, I could not write, teach, preach, speak, counsel, or do anything I am privileged to do for the Kingdom of God. Anything that I do for the Lord always involves my wife as the two of us are "one flesh." When godly submission is demonstrated in the husband/wife relationship, children can learn submission more easily. The opposite is also true. Few children learn proper biblical submission in a home with an unsubmissive wife.

Submission is not focused upon trusting another human being. My wife is not simply trusting me and thereby submitting to me as her husband. If anything, the opposite is true. My wife submits to me despite my sinful, flawed personhood. In reality, my wife is submitting to the Lord. Her submission to me and to any human authority is ultimately an act of her faith in submitting to the Lord Jesus Christ. Submission is trusting in the Person of Christ.

A nine year-old child named Becky learned to submit to her parents at an early age. On one occasion, Becky got out of the car and ran around the front toward her mother. Becky did not see a car backing out of the parking lot toward their car and it almost hit her. Her mother yelled, "Stop running, Becky. Look!" Just in time, Becky stopped and looked to see the car moving toward her. Because she had learned to hear the voice of her mother and obey, Becky was spared some serious physical consequences.

---

[56] Merriam-Webster, Inc. *Merriam-Webster's Collegiate Dictionary*. Includes Index. 10th ed. Springfield, Mass., U.S.A.: Merriam-Webster, 1996, c1993.

Sadly today, many people have trained their dogs to be under "voice command" but not their children. A German friend told me he was surprised to see that dogs were allowed in their restaurants as long as they were under "voice command." He said, "I know some pets in Germany that are under submission better than most children." These animals had been trained to listen and obey their masters while the children had not been trained to listen and obey their parents.

One evening when my children were little, I observed them running in a church building so I raised my voice just a little to get their attention. All I said was, "Hey!" They looked at me and I gave them a signal by waving both hands for all four of them to sit down. They sat down immediately and the person next to me said, "Wow! That was amazing." But as I thought about it, I realized that my children have learned to trust me because they know I want "good" for them! How much more does our heavenly Father want "good" for us and how much more does He know than we do! Teach your children to submit to the character of God.

Jesus trusted the Father so He submitted to Him. We may not understand God's reasoning or plans but we must trust Him by faith regardless. We must be like Jesus who basically said, "Not as I will, but as You will." If Jesus submitted to God, how much more are we to do so? Jesus was perfect and we are sinful; therefore, how much more must we trust Him?

I like to remind myself daily that God is my Owner. He created me. He redeemed me by the blood of Christ. He purchased me back from Satan. Therefore, He owns me and He is a good Master. I am not submitting to an evil Person! I am submitting to the most loving, gracious Person I have ever known, my Lord and Savior. However, in my flesh, I want to trust myself more than Christ. I know that my ways always get me into trouble and I know that His ways are life-giving. He is my Good Shepherd according to Psalm 23. I must trust Him and trust His Holy Word because my life is now hidden in Christ (Colossians 3:3).

As Christians we must embrace the truth that we are not our own, and that our ownership belongs to God. 1 Corinthians 6:19-20 writes this biblical truth in this manner: **"Or do you not know that your body is a temple of the Holy Spirit within you, whom you have from God? You are not your own, for you were bought with a price. So glorify God in your body."** Through the blood of Christ, you were purchased and redeemed back from Satan. In reality, everyone has an owner. We belong either to Satan or to God according to Jesus in John 8:44: **"You are of your father the devil, and your will is to do your father's desires. He was a murderer from the beginning, and has nothing to do with the truth, because there is no truth in him. When he lies, he speaks out of his own character, for he is a liar and the father of lies."**

You must teach your child that he is either owned by Satan, if he is not yet born again, or he is owned by the Lord. You must wrestle with this truth and understand that your job as a parent is to help your child see who his owner really is. He may think he is independent, in charge, and "the boss," but that is only a deception of Satan. Satan wants people to think that they are in charge of their lives. To serve self is to serve Satan. To serve Christ is to serve God who is the rightful Owner of all living creatures.

Conclusion

Teach your child to be submissive to God's Spirit and His Word. Teach him about the character of God found in Jesus Christ and the Bible. God has revealed His character to us, but only if we read and study the Scriptures can we come to understand it. In our flesh, we will very likely not see God and His divine character. In the flesh, we will only see ourselves, sin, suffering, sorrow, and death because **"the wages of sin is death"**; however, the good news is that **"the free gift of God is eternal life in Christ Jesus our Lord"** (Romans 3:23). Point your child to Christ and His free gift when you are teaching your child to submit to the will of the most loving Person in the universe: the Lord Jesus Christ.

KEY IDEAS AND PRACTICAL THINGS TO DO

1. Write out 10 practical ways you and your child can submit to your authorities.

2. Say "Not my will, but your will be done, Lord" for a week each time you face an adverse situation or circumstance.

3. Memorize Psalm 23 with your child. Pray this psalm out loud with your child. For example, "Thank you, Lord, that you are our Shepherd in that you take care of us and give us all of our needs..." Praying a psalm and making it apply to your own life is an excellent way to teach your child many things.

Chapter 25
Conclusion

Years later, at Edna's funeral, she was honored by her grandchildren who spoke fondly of her and her authentic walk with Christ. Though all of Edna's grandchildren have struggled with sin in their lives, they know that Christ's forgiveness and grace is sufficient to cover a multitude of their sins. They know the power of the Holy Spirit overcomes every temptation to sin, and offers a new, transformed life to those who diligently seek to know Jesus Christ!

There may not be a bigger challenge in life than biblical parenting. The concept of addiction-proof parenting is simple, but it requires a great deal of effort, attention, insight, and energy. It can best be done by committed followers of Christ who are empowered by the Holy Spirit and are thinking, speaking, and acting in accordance with God's Word. There are no shortcuts or easy methods.

Poor parenting has a price tag and you will either pay the price now or later in life. If you invest in this type of parenting while your children are young, you will reap many blessings. If you fail to invest now, you will likely suffer in the long-run.

People who are actively engaged in some type of addiction exhibit the five primary mentalities we have studied in this book. Recall that they progress in the following order: the entitlement mentality, the consumer mentality, the victim mentality, the perishing mentality, and the rebellious mentality. All five are destructive and interconnected. Your child's sinful nature will automatically formulate these sinful mentalities (or ways of thinking) if you are passive as a parent. It is your responsibility to help your children to interpret the events in their lives correctly and to respond biblically. You must help your children to re-interpret wrong ideas and thoughts about the Lord which are based upon their selfish, sinful nature, into thoughts that are accurate and biblical.

Assess your child now. Have you allowed him to think he is entitled to the material things and pleasures of this world? Is your child a consumer who seeks the next purchase or gift and lives by feelings rather than the commands of God? Is he in the victim mentality stage or has he progressed into the perishing mentality stage? If your child is in the rebellious mentality stage, you are in for a difficult time, but you can begin to reverse the cycle with solid, biblical parenting. Where is your child's state of mind? Is your child's thinking self-centered?

A bigger question is: "Where are you as a parent?" Are you fostering these mentalities in your children today? As mentioned previously, these mindsets feed the selfish nature and idolatrous desires for pleasure in your child. In reality, these mentalities lead to hopelessness and a life devoid of Christ.

The good news is that all of these detrimental mentalities can be replaced with the following fruit-producing mentalities: humility, giving, responsibility (obedience), gratitude (joy), and submission. Replacement and prevention occur through parents who are committed to parenting that will shape and transform the thinking of their children. You must parent God's way. The world's ideas of "good" parenting are often lies that must be rejected when they oppose the Word of God (Colossians 2:8). The world's "wisdom" is a collection of man's ideas that reinforce the mentalities mentioned above. Satan uses the lies of this world to promote his agenda and to lead people away from the truth. Satan simply wants people to act independently from God and His Word.

Satan will tempt your children to be their own bosses, as he tempted Adam and Eve in Genesis 3:5: **"For God knows that when you eat of it your eyes will be opened, and you will be like God, knowing good and evil."** Satan wants you to think you can be your own god and not be required to answer to anyone. Revelation 20:12 tells us that we will give an account to God in eternity: **"And I saw the dead, great and small, standing before the throne, and books were opened. Then another book was opened, which is the book of life. And the dead were judged by what was written in the books, according to what they had done."** As a parent, you will one day stand before the Lord and give an answer to Him for what you did or did not do as a parent of the children He gave to you. You are not their owner; but as parents you are the steward of your children. They belong to God, and He expects you to point them to Christ because they are His possessions. Do not lead them away from Christ, their Rightful Owner!

Do your words honor God? Do your thoughts esteem Him in His rightful place? Do your actions reflect the character of God accurately before your children? When you parent God's way, you will glorify God and benefit your children. God wants what is best for your children and He is a loving, "Abba, Father" who disciplines perfectly in love. Be like Him as much as you possibly can and learn when you make mistakes.

Being Like Christ

Addiction-Proof Parenting has a twofold purpose. First, this book is a call to trust God by being obedient to Him. Once you have identified the mentalities that can lead to addictive thinking, and the biblical antidotes found in Scripture, you must trust God by putting them into action. People say they trust God but often those are just words and not actions. This is the definition of hypocrisy. If God says it is a good thing to discipline your child with the rod and reproof, then heed His Word and obey Him. Trust God to use your discipline for your child's good and for His glory.

Second, this book is a call to discipleship. Many parents simply want to see their children converted to Christianity, which is a good goal; however, a better and more comprehensive goal is to see them strong in faith, which only comes through *intentional* discipleship of your child. Find opportunities every day to point your child to Christ and teach the Scriptures because they convey the love, truth, and justice of God. The Holy Spirit uses the Word of God to save God's children. Do your part to parent as well as you can and ask the Lord to graciously save your child's soul. Jesus told Nicodemus in John 3:8: **"The wind blows where it wishes, and you hear its sound, but you do not know where it comes from or where it goes. So it is with everyone who is born of the Spirit."** You must fight to keep truth in your own mind as well as in the minds of your children.

Sin of the Flesh vs. the Holy Spirit

At its core, addiction-proof parenting is not natural. Proverbs 28:26 says: **"Whoever trusts in his own mind is a fool, but he who walks in wisdom will be delivered."** You cannot parent in the flesh. You cannot parent with your own "wisdom" or with so-called "worldly wisdom." Instead, you must parent in the Holy Spirit's power and do what He leads you to do, which will always match His Word of truth.

It will do no good to read this book and not implement the biblical principles you have learned. You must walk in the wisdom of God and His Word. Find a way to use these principles in a practical way in your family today. Trust the Lord and do what is right in His eyes

187

because He can be trusted—even more than you can trust yourself! Ask for His forgiveness when you fail. Remember: God is true to His Word.

1 John 1:6-10 reminds us of God's character and reputation: **"If we say we have fellowship with him while we walk in darkness, we lie and do not practice the truth. But if we walk in the light, as he is in the light, we have fellowship with one another, and the blood of Jesus his Son cleanses us from all sin. If we say we have no sin, we deceive ourselves, and the truth is not in us. If we confess our sins, he is faithful and just to forgive us our sins and to cleanse us from all unrighteousness. If we say we have not sinned, we make him a liar, and his word is not in us."**

Glorify God today and do not "make Him a liar" (v.10 above); replace some of your bad parenting habits with good, addiction-proof parenting skills. Though very challenging, you can do this in the power of His might. The power that saves a soul from hell is the same power that will transform your parenting skills to be more like God's.

Slow your life down. Spend time in prayer and Bible study with your children. Teach them to appreciate God's handiwork in the world around you. Remind them of their fallen nature and constant need for Christ's sustaining power. Demonstrate to your child how God is present and active in every area of life.

Simplify your parenting strategy. Simply work on instilling humility, giving, responsibility, gratitude, and a submissive spirit in your child's mind. Review Matthew 22:37-40 and Ephesians 5:18-21 to help you remember the goals of addiction-proof parenting. Do not try to do too much. Focus upon your own thinking, language, and actions and your child will respond accordingly. If not, then ask your pastor, a leader in your church, a trusted Christian friend, or a biblical counselor to help you.[57]

Most important, parenting provides many opportunities to advance the kingdom of heaven by cultivating your child's relationship with Christ. Parenting provides many opportunities to glorify our great Father in Heaven who is our perfect Parent. He alone is worthy of all praise, glory, and honor. Parent your child in the love of Christ, fully trusting in Him to reveal Himself as the God of love to your child today.

---

[57] Go to www.nanc.org to find a list of biblical counselors in your area.

Appendices

Appendix A
The Whole Story

I put one paragraph of this entire story at the beginning of each chapter in the book. If you would like to read it in its entirety, I've included it for you here. I would like you to read it now and then to answer some of the questions listed at the end that are designed to provoke additional thinking.

God's Transforming Power

Young Scott is being raised by his grandparents who love him very much. They feel sorry for "Scottie" as they call him because his father died from an overdose of drugs and his mother is on crystal meth. Since they feel sorry for "Scottie," they tend to give him everything he wants. "Well, he doesn't see his parents so maybe we can give him the things he wants" is what his grandparents often think.

At school, young "Scottie" is known simply as "Scott." This day Scott quickly darts out of his last class and heads toward the school gymnasium. A circle of his best friends are standing there and they welcome him to the group. He talks to them for just a little while before heading behind the gym. Scott knows he doesn't have much time to meet Derrick before catching his school bus home to his grandparents' house. Behind their school gym, Scott sells a bag of marijuana to Derrick who quickly hides it in his backpack...

When Derrick gets home after football practice, he quickly unloads his backpack in his bedroom and begins rolling several cigarettes with the marijuana he bought from Scott. His mother yells, "Derrick, dinner is ready. Come, eat." Derrick doesn't respond and continues making "joints" to take with him to the big party tonight. Fifteen minutes later, Derrick's mother bursts into his room with one earring in her hand and the other in her ear saying, "Derrick, go eat before the food gets any colder." She notices the rolling papers and drugs and says, "Derrick, you better get rid of that stuff by the time I get back from my date tonight! I'm leaving now—my boyfriend's here." She turns and rushes out of his room and out of the front door.

191

Derrick arrives at Freddie's house. He is the star football player and this is his eighteenth birthday party. Derrick sees his friend, Raymond, getting out of his car with four girls he drove to the party. "Hey, Raymond," Derrick whispers, "I brought some good stuff I got from Scott for us—for later." They go inside at the same time as someone excitedly announces, "The keg is in the backyard, Guys!" The drinking begins at Freddie's house while his parents are away at the lake for the weekend.

After drinking for awhile, Derrick and Raymond smoke a marijuana cigarette with some of the other boys in a back bedroom. They laugh and lose track of time while taking turns playing violent video games that belong to Freddie. Popping his head in the room, Freddie says to Derrick and Raymond, "When you guys get done with that game, come out here with me. I want you to meet somebody." Derrick and Raymond quit playing the game and meet Freddie's new friend, Matt, who introduces the boys to a new drug, Adderall.®

Matt has taken Adderall® since being diagnosed with ADHD in the fifth grade when his parents went through a divorce and Matt struggled to sit still in class. Not knowing what to do, Matt's mom took him to a psychiatrist who prescribed the medication for him. Now, Matt likes to take his own Adderall and buys more of it from other friends who have the same ADHD diagnosis but do not like to take Adderall. Matt has enough to share with Derrick, Raymond, and Freddie who are already drinking alcohol and smoking pot at the party.

At the party, Matt and Freddie leave Derrick and Raymond who offer a marijuana cigarette to the four girls Raymond brought to the party. Three of the girls smoke a joint together but Edna, the fourth girl, says "No, thanks." Edna remembered that her parents literally said that they would "kill her" if they ever caught her drinking or drugging.

Edna wants to go home from the party but she sees that her ride, Raymond, has already become too intoxicated to drive home. Edna's friends encourage her to "just try it with us one time" referring to the marijuana. "Its fun," one friend said, "and it will make you giggle a lot." Edna looks at her friends and considers it for a minute. "My parents are always asleep when I get home anyway," she thinks to herself.

Walking past Edna, two of the boys, Freddie and Matt, are joking and pushing each other. They are holding water balloons and preparing to throw them into a big group of people who are standing around the keg. Launching the balloons, the circle scatters with several people getting soaked. Freddie and Matt laugh hysterically until two guys from that broken circle come running after them and tackle them. Freddie and Matt find themselves on the ground in a wrestling match with the two guys at the side of the house.

While their two buddies are in a fight outside, Derrick and Raymond are inside the house and back to smoking pot with some of their other friends. Derrick tells Raymond he doesn't like the way the Adderall makes him feel, but Raymond says he loves it and wishes he could take another pill or two. Raymond says he is going to see if he can go to the psychiatrist to get diagnosed with ADHD so that he can get a prescription for Adderall.

Before long, Derrick tells Raymond that his chest is really hurting. "Maybe I shouldn't have taken those Adderall," Derrick says. "I feel terrible." Raymond blows off Derrick's comment by saying, "Don't be a big baby." Derrick walks away from Raymond and is beginning to stumble. Falling to the floor, Derrick lands on his face as one of the girls at the party screams. Someone calls 911 and the paramedics are en route.

Edna, who is fifteen years old, takes the joint from one of her three girlfriends. She hurriedly walks outside to the front porch as they follow her. Edna pauses for a brief moment yet puts the joint to her mouth and inhales for a few seconds. Her friends giggle with glee as Edna smokes. However, their laughing stops abruptly when a set of bright lights shines in their eyes and a man's voice shouts, "Stop right there, young ladies. I'm Detective Smith with the police department. You are under arrest."

It takes several guys to break up the fight between Freddie, Matt, and the two other guys. Freddie has a bloody nose and Matt is holding his right arm. Both boys look badly beaten with bruises, cuts, rips in their clothing, and blood smeared on their faces. In the background, Freddie hears a siren and panics. His only words are "Oh, no!" as he briskly walks toward the front porch of his house where he suddenly sees flashing blue lights and the police holding Edna by the arm.

The paramedics pull up to the front of the house and are directed to Derrick who is lying unconscious on the living room floor. They begin CPR and moments later decide to take Derrick to the hospital. Raymond, Freddie, Matt, and the others watch as Derrick remains unconscious and is loaded into the ambulance.

Derrick's mother is contacted by the police. When she arrives at the hospital, Derrick is already dead from cardiac arrest. He could not be revived. The toxic mix of large amounts of alcohol, marijuana, and Adderall were too much for his young body to handle. It was the most severe consequence a seventeen year old boy could experience from one night of so-called "partying" and "fun."

It was the most difficult phone call Edna ever had to make. She wondered who else she could call besides her parents but no one came to mind. She sat and stared at the phone for what seemed like an eternity. Dialing the number was surreal until her Dad said, "Hello?" Edna cried out a weak, "Daddy, it's me. I'm so sorry" and that was all she could say as she wept on the phone for a few moments.

Needless to say, Edna's parents were devastated as they sat in the juvenile detention center. "We thought we raised you better than this, Edna" was the last thing Edna heard them say as she was escorted to her juvenile cell. Edna's parents decided to allow her to experience the consequences from her poor choices and Edna never tried alcohol or drugs again in her life.

Freddie's parents were called in the middle of the night to return home from their lake house. Freddie confessed everything to his parents who were disappointed in their son's poor choices; however, because they had a relationship with Christ, Freddie's parents understood forgiveness. Freddie's parents held him responsible for his sinful choices and provided for him to meet with a biblical counselor. Through this process of biblical counseling, Freddie experienced the forgiveness of Christ personally, made a profession of faith in Christ, and surrendered his life to be lived for the glory of God.

Both sets of parents for Matt and Raymond took an inactive role in their child's upbringing. Matt continued to abuse Adderall and Raymond continued to abuse alcohol and marijuana. Both boys went to college but Matt flunked out and took a job working as a waiter in a restaurant. Raymond made it through college, became an attorney, and makes a successful living in the eyes of the world eyes even though he smokes marijuana almost daily.

After Derrick's death, his mother sought help for her grief from the church down the street from where she lived. Little did she know at that time, but the church offered biblical counseling free of charge. They showed her love and compassion and evangelized her with the Gospel so that she received forgiveness of her sin and freedom from her guilt. Derrick's mother repented of her sins of omission (failing to parent Derrick) and was reconciled to Christ through biblical counseling.

It is now ten years after Derrick's death. His mother is teaching younger women to love their children by being active, biblical parents who discipline consistently and lovingly. The Lord has been gracious to her by allowing her to remarry a godly man and to raise two children with her new husband. Both of these children are walking with the Lord Jesus in an intimate relationship and she is grateful to have been an instrument of righteousness in the Hands of Christ.

As an adult now with her own family, Edna recognizes the importance of spending time in relationship with her children. She knew her parents loved her, but she never felt close and connected to them. She feared them, but that fear never kept her from making poor choices. Though she only tried marijuana that one time, she paid a heavy price for it. When she was younger she struggled with an eating "addiction." She would battle over-eating and sometimes purging for many years until she sought help from her pastor and his wife.

Edna's children grew strong in their Christian faith. They learned how to think biblically through both of their parents' strong teaching of God's Word and their parents' faithful commitment to live according to these biblical principles. Their relationship with their parents was unique because they felt free to tell their parents anything, even about their sinful choices, and they would still be accepted and loved even though they knew they must still face the consequences of their choices. Their faith in Christ was real, relational, and thriving as they passed on their faith to their children.

Years later, at Edna's funeral, she was honored by her grandchildren who spoke fondly of her and her authentic walk with Christ. Though all of Edna's grandchildren have struggled with sin in their lives, they know that Christ's forgiveness and grace is sufficient to cover a multitude of their sins. They know the power of the Holy Spirit overcomes every temptation to sin, and offers a new, transformed life to those who diligently seek to know Jesus Christ!

The End

Now, let's do a little exercise: Who was most responsible for Edna's drug usage? In the space provided below, rank the following people from "most responsible" to "least responsible" for Edna's drug use: Derrick, Scott, Derrick's mother, Raymond, Freddie, Freddie's parents, Matt, the 3 girlfriends, Edna, and Edna's parents.

	NAME	REASON
1. Most Responsible		
2.		
3.		
4.		
5.		
6.		
7.		
8.		
9.		
10. Least Responsible		

Would your answers above change if I added the phrase: "According to the Bible, who was most responsible for Edna's drug usage?" Who does God hold most responsible for her drug usage?

	NAME	REASON
1. Most Responsible		
2.		
3.		
4.		
5.		
6.		
7.		
8.		
9.		
10. Least Responsible[58]		

---

[58] MY CORRECT ANSWERS: Edna, Derrick, the 3 girlfriends, Raymond, Freddie, Derrick's mother, Scott, Edna's parents, Freddie's parents, and Matt. Some of these are interchangeable but Edna must come first as she is responsible for herself no matter what temptations to sin appeared to her!

MORE QUESTIONS FOR THOUGHT:

1. What mentality did Scott's grandparents unwittingly foster in him?

2. What do you think was Derrick's mother's primary focus in the beginning? How did her focus change?

3. Do you think most adults would have thought of these young people as "good kids"? Why or why not?

4. Is Matt's diagnosis legitimate? What scientific studies verify that medications prescribed to treat ADHD actually yield the desired results of improved performance in school? See if you can find any studies to support it. (Most parents say that they give their child the meds so that the child will do better in school but where is the scientific evidence that supports this desired result?)

5. Did it anger you to think that Matt and Raymond never learned their lessons and that Raymond is successful in the world's eyes?

6. What were Edna's 3 girlfriends' roles in all of this? Could they have been a positive influence rather than a negative one (1 Corinthians 15:33)?

7. How active do you think all of the parents were in their children's lives? Do you think these parents were too passive or are kids 'just going to be kids'? How much training and preparation can parents give their children?

8. Did Derrick's death seem sudden to you? Isn't that how these things happen? How can you instruct your child about the side effects of medications and the dangers of taking any medication that belongs to someone else?

9. What life lessons did each character learn from this tragedy?

10. What did Edna learn through all of this? How did God use this one event in Edna's life to redeem her life and also the lives of her grandchildren?

Appendix B
Knowledge, Understanding and Wisdom

Teaching your children the Bible is not an easy task; however, many parents think they must have a seminary degree in order to teach Bible basics to their children and that is not true. In the following appendix, I want to encourage you to teach your child the Word of God in a simple way. The three "R's" of learning are "repetition, repetition, and repetition," so do not be afraid to repeat yourself.

As a parent, begin by familiarizing your child with the books of the Bible. Children can memorize the books of the Bible either put to a song or by rote memory depending upon their age. Teach your children the basics of how to navigate through the Bible using the chapters and verses. They can begin to memorize small verses of Scripture, especially when coupled with music.

A fantastic resource we use is found at www.biblebee.org called "The National Bible Bee." It is like a spelling bee except that it is centered upon the Bible. It is a free curriculum as of this writing and contains Bible memory verses, explanations, Bible knowledge quiz cards, overviews of books of the Bible, and more. You do not have to enter the Bible Bee to use this resource and it is a tremendous help for parents and children alike because of the excellent teaching and explanations.

Give your children a working knowledge of the Bible. Then, once that is established, teach them to understand the concepts of the Scriptures. Many people think the Bible is impossible to understand but that simply is not true. While you may not understand portions of Scripture fully, you can teach what you do understand. Apply the Word to your child's life in a practical manner. To do this effectively, you must be learning the Bible for yourself.

Some easy verses to teach and apply to real life situations are as follows: Romans 12:21, Ephesians 4:22-24, Proverbs 3:5-6, Genesis 1:26-27, James 1:22, Matthew 4:17, Matthew 6:7-14, Matthew 6:19-20, Matthew 6:33, and Philippians 4:8. Your children must understand that the Word of God is connected to their lives in practical ways. The Bible is life-giving and enables us to live our lives victoriously.

Finally, wisdom comes from applying biblical principles. In other words, wisdom comes from "doing" the Bible and leads to blessing. James 1:22-25 states: **"But be doers of the word, and not hearers only, deceiving yourselves. For if anyone is a hearer of the word and not a doer, he is like a man who looks intently at his natural face in a mirror. For he looks at himself and goes away and at once forgets what he was like. But the one who looks into the perfect law, the law of liberty, and perseveres, being no hearer who forgets but a doer who acts, he will be blessed in his doing."** Ephesians 4:22-24 encourages us to put-on "doing the right things" that please Christ which must replace the put-offs that are not pleasing to Him and lead to problems in our lives. Transformation is God's best for your child so teach your child what not to do as well as what to do. In other words, teach your children to be new creations in Christ.

Remember to help your children to have a basic knowledge, deeper understanding, and applied wisdom of the Holy Scriptures. Start slowly and watch them grow in these areas in a very short time. You will be amazed at how quickly children can learn the Bible.

Appendix C
Mark & Mary's Tips for Parents

Many people comment about how well behaved our children are and we are quick to say that all of the glory belongs to the Lord because we are parents with human frailties. Thankfully, He alone is THE faithful parent that your children and mine need. Nevertheless, Mary and I have found the following tips to be helpful to us. We hope and pray that they will be helpful to you!

We patterned our tips according to the four areas of development of Jesus in Luke 2:52, **"And Jesus increased in wisdom and in stature and in favor with God and man."** Jesus grew in wisdom (intellectually), in stature (physically), in favor with God (spiritually), and in favor with man (socially). Therefore, our tips are going to be divided into these four areas: intellectually, physically, spiritually, and socially.

INTELLECTUALLY
- We limit video games, television, and the internet. Our children do not have unlimited access to these things. We limit these things to weekends and then only for a few hours.
- Our children spend more time reading books each week than they do watching television.
- We home school our children primarily because we can teach to their strengths and weaknesses. This goes for all four areas: intellectually, physically, spiritually and socially.
- Teach your children how to research and find sources of information. Wise persons know where to find information.
- Find God-fearing, good teachers for your children in areas where you are weak intellectually.

PHYSICALLY
- Consult a nutritionist to learn how to prepare healthy foods and serve correct portions. At restaurants and at home, we only let our children drink water or milk. Now, they love it and choose it over soft drinks.

- Give your children no choices at restaurants. Order their drinks (i.e. water) and food for them. This is easier than it sounds. All you do is set the standard and stick to it. Then you have no arguments.

- At home, feed your children what you want them to eat. Do not prepare three different meals for three different children.

- We tell our children, "you do not have to like it; you just have to eat it." We often try to stay at the table as encouragers to one who may be having difficulty with a new food like broccoli. Sibling encouragement is powerful.

- Regular bed times are always best. While we are often unsuccessful at establishing regular bed times, we recommend 8:00 p.m. but it all depends on when you rise in the morning. Pediatricians are in agreement that most children are sleep deprived. Make an effort to change this. Ask your pediatrician how much sleep your child needs. A wise teacher once told us this memorable maxim: "Sleep in on the front end," meaning that if you are sleep deprived, go to bed earlier, instead of sleeping later in the morning. Let's apply this to your children's schedules.

- We encourage our children to play outside rather than watch television or play video games.

SPIRITUALLY

- Pray with your child because that is how they learn to pray. Teach him to pray short, one-sentence prayers for others. Again, we home school because we want our children to know Christ. Knowing Him is our first priority.

- Teach your child that prayer is talking to God and that God talks to us through His Word by the Holy Spirit. Reading the Word is how God primarily reveals Himself to us and speaks to us.

- Have a time each week of singing praises to God. Use a CD or play an instrument like a piano or guitar if you are able.

- Have a fun time of acting out Bible stories in a game of "charades."

- Assign your child to read a chapter of Proverbs for each corresponding day of the month (i.e. 17th chapter on the 17th day of the month). Discuss it with your child at night.

SOCIALLY

- Encourage interaction with others but do not fall into the thinking that very little children "need" friends. Young children do not need friends when they are between the ages of two and four years old. Instead, they need a mother who structures their day, disciplines them, and teaches them why God placed them here.

- Teach your children to interact appropriately with their siblings. Do not allow older siblings to torment, make fun of, mock, "pick on," discipline, or disrespect a younger sibling (and vice versa!). Make your home one that emphasizes honor toward each member of your family.

- Protect your child by choosing your child's friends. Get to know the parents and family of your child's friends before you have the child over to spend the night. (We do not allow 'sleep-overs' away from home!)

- Promote and provide for your children to engage often in social interactions with strong Christian adults. Hold the standard high. You will be pleasantly surprised at what they are capable of discussing. Then provide opportunities to discuss these interactions later teaching values and biblical principles at that time.

Conclusion

Many of these things might seem extreme or harsh depending upon your upbringing and point of reference. We are to be in the world but not of the world, which is a difficult challenge. We cannot leave the world so we must teach our children to deal with the temptations, sufferings, struggles, and problems of this world. Children must be trained to plan ahead and know what to do when challenging situations arise.

Appendix D
God's Grace for Parents Who Think They Have Failed

You may be reading this book and wondering: "My children are adults now. What if I have already blown it as a parent? What do I do now?" If your children are no longer under your authority, then there is still much for you to do. First, you can pray and ask the Lord for His grace and mercy. Quite simply, grace is getting what you do not deserve and mercy is not getting what you do deserve. Humble yourself in prayer before the Lord according to James 4:6b: **"Therefore it says, 'God opposes the proud, but gives grace to the humble.'"** If there is sin involved, then confess your sin and ask for God's forgiveness. 1 John 1:9 assures you: **"If we confess our sins, he is faithful and just to forgive us our sins and to cleanse us from all unrighteousness."** Forgiveness does not mean that you might not experience more consequences. King David repented after his sin of adultery and the Lord forgave him, yet one of the consequences of his sin was the death of the baby who was born of the adultery (2 Samuel 12:15-23).

Following are some suggestions for you to concentrate on and pray about:

1. <u>Intentionally focus your thinking upon His grace and mercy rather than beating yourself up about your failures and shortcomings</u>. God is sovereign and He is love (1 John 4:18), so plead for His redemptive power in the lives of your children. Do not blame God for wrong-doing or bitterness will creep into your heart and poison you. Instead, be like Job after his great loss of personal possessions and his children in Job 1:21-22: **"And he said, 'Naked I came from my mother's womb, and naked shall I return. The LORD gave, and the LORD has taken away; blessed be the name of the LORD.' In all this Job did not sin or charge God with wrong."**

2. <u>Look for the good in your circumstances</u>. God is a Redeemer, meaning that He makes good from what is bad. Make a list of things that God has done and is doing in your child's life and another list of prayerful hopes you want Him to do in your particular situation. Philippians 4:8 says: **"Finally, brothers, whatever is true, whatever is honorable, whatever is just, whatever is pure, whatever is lovely,**

whatever is commendable, if there is any excellence, if there is anything worthy of praise, think about these things." Use this verse to help you develop your list of God's redemptive power in your situation. Look for things to be grateful for and do not allow a spirit of bitterness to infect you as Hebrews 12:15 reminds you: "See to it that no one fails to obtain the grace of God; that no 'root of bitterness' springs up and causes trouble, and by it many become defiled." Bitterness grows in a person's heart, spreading like a "root" and defiling many others. No one wants to be around a bitter person so you must purpose in your heart to fight the temptation to be bitter, hurt, and disappointed. Do this by looking for God's redemptive good. Be a "praiser" of God rather than a "complainer."

3. Ask several of your friends to meet with you for a time of focused prayer for your child. Meet regularly to pray together to build a support system. Be sure to pick wise friends who are not gossips! Do not be afraid to discuss your situation openly with this group as you may be surprised at how they have experienced similar circumstances. Meet weekly or at least monthly and spend this time in focused prayer.

4. Once you have strong prayer support, ask someone in your church to evangelize your lost loved one. Consider the possibility of asking the church to send a team of two or more persons to meet with your loved one to gently call them to repentance. You could call your loved one to repentance yourself, but it might not be received well coming from you for whatever reason. Repentance is a gift of God and the Holy Spirit gives this gift to whomever He chooses (Romans 2:4).

5. Never give up. Trust God and give it to Him by laying your loved one at the foot of the cross. When you do that you demonstrate that you trust in His plan for your loved one's life over your best plans. Be creative in your prayer life. Ask Him to send messengers of the Gospel to cross the path of your loved ones. Ask Him to bring consequences into your loved one's life to lead them to repentance and a right relationship with Christ. We are too often inclined to pray for God's blessing and protection for our children, but it is through suffering and difficult circumstances that people see their need of a Savior. Ask God to make Himself known in daily occurrences of your loved one's life. Pray consistently and be specific in your requests to God. Pray with boldness, trusting God to do His holy will in your situation.

6. <u>Help others less fortunate than you to prevent bitterness and a bad attitude in your heart</u>. Stay active in your church or in a local Christian ministry. Focus your efforts upon helping others who are less fortunate than you. For example, visit a children's hospital, an orphanage, a group home, a nursing home, and the like. There are always situations worse than yours and it helps to keep your problems and hopes in proper perspective.

There are few things more difficult for parents than watching their children and grandchildren adversely affected by the poor choices they made as parents or by the way they neglected their parental responsibilities. If this is your situation, you must remember two simultaneous truths: God is sovereign and man is responsible.

Let's look at God's sovereignty. God is in control of everything, so trust Him. Ask Him to divinely intervene in your circumstances in His way according to His timing. Too many parents make the mistake of trying to fix their mistakes in their own strength and by their own limited power and resources. They often end up spending too much money on trying to fix an unwilling heart. John 6:64 reminds us that human effort in the flesh is worthless: **"It is the Spirit who gives life; the flesh is of no avail. The words that I have spoken to you are spirit and life."** Notice that the power is in the Holy Spirit Who gives life to your lost loved one. Also, notice the connection between the Spirit and Christ's words. Do not be afraid to share the Gospel with your children in creative ways when you have an opportunity because Romans 10:17 states: **"So faith comes from hearing, and hearing through the word of Christ."** Your loved one must hear the word of Christ, so present His Words in a winsome, loving way rather than in a judging way. Let the Holy Spirit bring conviction and judgment; not you.

It is a delicate balance to be sure. For more insights, I recommend my book, *Divine Intervention: Hope and Help for Families of Addicts*. This book was written to give loved ones some practical things to do and challenge them to wait upon the Lord by faith. At the end of the day, all of this rests on faith in the sovereignty of God. Do you trust the Lord? Can He be trusted with your loved ones?

Now, let's look at man's responsibility. Your offspring are responsible for their choices. I know of situations where terrible families produced great Christians and I know where the opposite occurred—great Christian families produced terrible children. Remember that the Fifth Commandment in Exodus 20:12 is directed toward your children, not you. Your child must honor you whether he likes it or not. No one is a perfect parent so do not allow your children to blame you for their sinful choices. There is never an excuse to sin and make wrong choices. You may have been the worst parent in your town, but that is not an excuse for your children to continue in sin. Confess your sins to your child and ask for forgiveness and reconciliation of the relationship. If your child is not interested, then it is likely that he has unforgiveness in his heart.

If your child is willing, I strongly recommend that you seek biblical counseling to help you both have a healthier relationship. Parents who "enable" their children to keep sinning are only prolonging the agony by reinforcing the wrong behavior. If the child continues to manipulate, deceive, and use your resources, then you are encouraging them to continue in the "addiction" of choice. You are actually undermining the very goal that you wish to accomplish: helping your child to become free from the trap of "addiction." What child will ever change if he has unlimited resources to continue? The answer is not many.

The following section may sound harsh but it is the truth. Some people call it "tough love." In fact, I have had many "thank you" emails and letters from parents who basically told me, "I followed the biblical parameters in your *Divine Intervention* book and after a period of time, my child came back to me with a truly repentant heart and remorseful attitude. We now have a right relationship. Praise God!" Here is the loving but seemingly "harsh" truth: In faith, turn your child over to Satan and this world's system for the purpose of allowing your child to come back to Christ after making poor choices and experiencing harsh consequences. Do not do this out of anger or hurt or fear, but do this out of faith in a sovereign God who loves mankind enough to hold us responsible. Your choice to do this is an act of faith and trust in the power and goodness of God, the Perfect Parent and "Abba" Father.

Biblical examples of turning over to Satan a professing Christian who continues in sin and acts like an unbeliever are mentioned in two places of Scripture. First, in 1 Timothy 1:19-20, the Apostle Paul comments on two persons who rejected the faith so he allowed them to go and experience their rejection of God in the hope that they would return back to Christ: **"holding faith and a good conscience. By rejecting this, some have made shipwreck of their faith, among whom are Hymenaeus and Alexander, whom I have handed over**

to Satan that they may learn not to blaspheme." Paul wanted them to learn not to blaspheme God. He was more concerned about their relationship with God and God's glory than he was about anything else. That is the goal and attitude you must have in regard to your child or children.

God's glory must be most important to you. Is God's glory being dragged through the mud by your disobedient, unwilling child? If so, then you must be like the church in 1 Corinthians 5:5 who were commanded to put a sexual sinner out of their church fellowship for the purpose of saving his soul: **"you are to deliver this man to Satan for the destruction of the flesh, so that his spirit may be saved in the day of the Lord."** God's glory is important to God and it must be so to you. God is not pleased with those who profess to love Him yet act sinfully and in an unloving way toward others. This man in 1 Corinthians 5 was polluting the church body and shaming God by his willful disobedience. The church was warned to remove this man from their fellowship for a period of time where the lusts of his "flesh" would be destroyed so that his soul and spirit might be saved. The Bible makes clear the fact that the choice is upon the man in this situation; it says he **"may be saved,"** not presumptuously that he "will be definitely saved." It was an act of faith on their part to trust God because they obviously loved this man and did not want to ask him to leave their fellowship.

One of the greatest testimonies of a rebellious child who came back to the Lord is Billy Graham's son, Franklin. Now, by God's grace and powerful Hand, Franklin Graham, though not a perfect man, is serving the Lord and serving others. Billy Graham experienced great suffering and heartache through a difficult period of his child's rebellion; however, he is thankful to God for His plan for Franklin's life in both this life and in the eternal life to come. So, have you sinned? Then, follow Proverbs 28:13: **"Whoever conceals his transgressions will not prosper, but he who confesses and forsakes them will obtain mercy."** Forsaking your transgressions and sin may mean that by faith in God you now turn your child over to the pleasures of this world and to Satan for a period of time where God will work His sovereign plan in your child's life.

ABOUT THE AUTHOR

Dr. Mark E. Shaw is the Founder and President of Truth in Love Ministries, an equipping and counseling ministry which operates through local churches using an innovative team approach to ministry. Dr. Shaw desires to see local churches of the Lord Jesus strengthened by teaching and equipping leaders and called lay persons to competently provide shepherding care for God's "flock" of children (1 Peter 5:2) and by speaking the truth in love to one another (Ephesians 4:15).

Dr. Shaw earned both a Doctor of Ministry in Biblical Counseling and a Master of Arts in Biblical Studies from Birmingham Theological Seminary. He also obtained a Master of Science in Educational Psychology from Florida State University, and a Bachelor of Arts in Psychology from the University of South Alabama.

He holds biblical counseling certification with the National Association of Nouthetic Counselors (NANC) since 2002, and is a certified Master's Level Addiction Professional (MLAP) with the Alabama Association of Drug and Alcohol Addiction since 1999.

For nearly two decades, he has supervised and trained counselors in marriage and family counseling, addictions counseling, and most recently in biblical counseling. In addition to counseling in the local church, he has worked as a director and counselor in outpatient clinics, crisis residential programs, intensive outpatient programs, residential rehabilitation programs, and inpatient adolescent group homes. He has witnessed the transforming and reconciling power of the Lord Jesus Christ in the lives of the many people he has served over the years.

Dr. Shaw's familiarity with biblical truths and the fallacies of many psychological theories enables him to have a unique perspective to frequently speak the truth in love to individuals, married couples, and families. Dr. Shaw and his wife, Mary, have four children and reside near Birmingham, Alabama.

For more information on **Truth in Love Ministries**, please visit www.histruthinlove.org.